Duct Tape
Discovery Workshop
Easy & Stylish Duct Tape Designs

Tonia Jenny

NORTH LIGHT BOOKS
Cincinnati, Ohio
ArtistsNetwork.com

Contents

Introduction [4]

Chapter 1
Basic Techniques [6]

Chapter 2
Fashionable Accessories [12]

Chapter 3
Cards and Gifts [54]

Visit **artistsnetwork.com/ducttapediscovery** for more duct tape discoveries.

Introduction

One single roll of duct tape holds such promise! Much like the possibilities inherent in one skein of yarn or one yard of fabric, once you learn a few basic techniques for working with duct tape (and there really are just a few), the sky truly is the limit. Need a new wallet? Make one from duct tape. Want some new earrings? Make some from duct tape. Wishing you had some trendy coasters for your next party? You guessed it . . . make them from duct tape!

From fashion-forward accessories to sweet and thoughtful gifts; from items to decorate your home to accessories you can use on the go, I know you're going to want to get started today seeing exactly what you can do with duct tape and how easy it is to do it.

Creating these projects really was a journey of discovery for me. I learned that the creative muscle can be pretty prolific when the options are kept to a minimum. To me this meant sticking to tape (no pun intended) as my primary material and carefully deciding if additional items such as paper, plastic or notions were truly necessary before including them. Each of these projects is really all about the impressive quality of duct tape and its ability to offer you, the creator, the freedom to make just about anything you can dream up. From my experience, if it can be made from paper or fabric or several other flexible materials, it can probably be crafted in duct tape.

The things you create with duct tape can be as attractive and as functional as you want them to be. Hopefully this book will get your wheels turning, and you'll be inspired to not only create what's in the book, but also to put your own spin on things and maybe even design some projects of your own. Give one project a try and then stick with it!

Chapter 1
Basic Techniques

Yes, working with duct tape is a sticky business. The good news is that you really need to know only a few things about working with duct tape to make great-looking projects. You'll also need just a couple of tools to complete everything in this book:

- cutting mat with a ruled grid (preferably 18" × 24" [46cm × 61cm]) or larger

- craft knife and no. 11 replacement blades

- metal straightedge

- duct tape (no projects in the book require more than one full roll per color)

For projects you'll want to embellish with duct tape (such as circles, letters or other designs), you'll also need:

- pencil and parchment paper or

- Spellbinders die-cutting system (optional)

To cut many of the embellishment shapes for the projects, I used a nifty die-cutting system from Spellbinders. I don't know that other systems would work with the stickiness of the tape, but I had great results with Spellbinders. Alternatively, you can certainly cut shapes by hand.

Additional items may vary per project (sometimes you'll use eyelets, beads, shrink plastic, jewelry wire and so on), but the call for these items is fairly minimal.

For a list of resources, visit artistsnetwork.com/ducttapediscovery.

Single-Sided Fabric

A single-sided fabric is one that is left sticky on the back so you can attach it to something else or something else can be attached to it.

MATERIALS LIST

cutting mat

craft knife

duct tape

straightedge

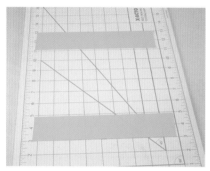

1 Decide what size fabric you'll need. For this example, a piece 8" × 10" (20cm × 25cm).

Cut one strip of the tape slightly longer than 8" (20cm) and place it along one line on the cutting mat. Cut a second strip about the same length and position it on the mat so the outside edge is 10" (25cm) from the outside edge of the first strip.

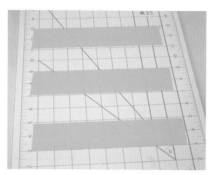

2 Place a third piece centered between the first two.

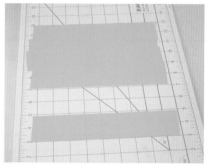

3 Fill in the remaining spaces evenly with strips of tape. Layer them on top of each other with at least ½" (13mm) of overlap.

TIP: Keeping the spacing even between your layers means the visible ridges in the fabric will be even as well.

4 Aligning the straightedge along the marks that will give you the width you need—in this case, 8" (20cm)—trim the scraggly edges using a straightedge and a craft knife.

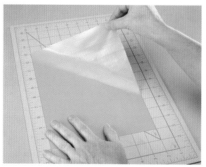

5 Using the tip of a craft knife, start to remove the fabric from one corner. It should peel up in one piece. This is a single-sided sheet of duct tape fabric.

Visit **artistsnetwork.com/ducttapediscovery** for more duct tape discoveries.

Double-Sided Fabric

A lot of projects begin with a double-sided piece of fabric. Think of these pieces as the individual elements you'd cut from fabric or paper to create something.

MATERIALS LIST

cutting mat

craft knife

duct tape

straightedge

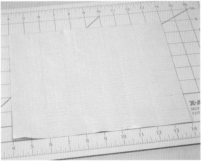

1 To create a double-sided sheet of fabric, begin with a single-sided piece cut to the dimension you need and position it so it's aligned with the rules on the cutting mat, sticky side up.

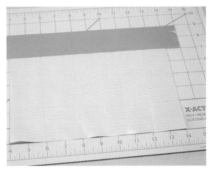

2 Cut one strip of tape slightly longer than the fabric and run it perpendicular to the direction of the strips on the first piece of fabric.

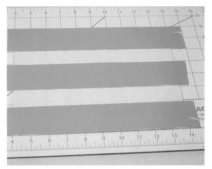

3 Place a second strip of tape at the bottom to help keep the fabric in place. Place another strip in the middle.

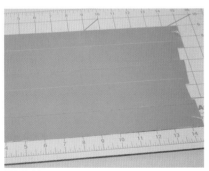

4 Fill in the remaining areas with evenly spaced strips of tape.

5 Trim the edges with a straightedge and a craft knife.

Half-Width Tape

To cut down on as much wasted tape as possible, I often use a half-width of tape rather than a specific measurement. The width of a standard roll of tape is just under 2" (5cm), so rather than provide a measurement of $^{15}/_{16}$" (2.38cm), I made it easier on all of us by simply using "half-width."

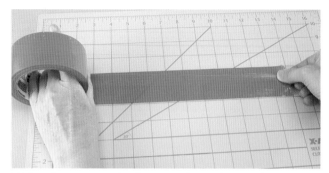 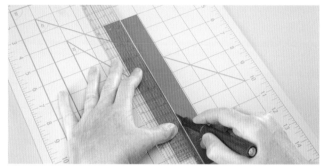

1 Visually center a strip of tape on the cutting mat between the rules for 2" (5cm). You should have about $^1/_{16}$" (2mm) on each side of the tape before the lines.

2 Trim the tape to the length it needs to be. Cut the tape in half using the center rule line. You now have two half-widths of tape.

Patterned Tape

Some varieties of patterned tape are printed in such a way that if you overlap the tape at the right spot, your pattern continues seamlessly. To see if a tape you're working with does this, pull out a 24" (61cm) or so length and determine whether the pattern appears to repeat. If it does, you should be able to quickly tell if one side of the tape matches up with the other.

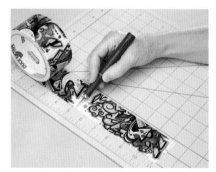  

1 Some patterned tapes can be lined up to create a whole picture, like this graffiti tape.

Using the image on the tape roll label, find the first section of the image and place it on your cutting mat.

2 The next section of tape should be the next section of the image. Carefully line it up with the first section of tape.

3 As you line up the images, the tape should overlap by about $^1/_8$" (3mm). Because of this overlap, some tape will be wasted by creating these patterns.

Visit artistsnetwork.com/ducttapediscovery for more duct tape discoveries.

Working on Parchment Paper

If you don't have a roll of parchment paper in your pantry already, you're going to want to pick some up today. Parchment paper makes cutting shapes from duct tape far easier than cutting them on a cutting mat alone. By using parchment paper, you can achieve much more detail as well as easily transfer a pattern or hand-drawn element.

MATERIALS LIST

parchment paper
pencil
duct tape
craft knife
cutting mat

1 Write your word or design on a piece of parchment paper using a pencil.

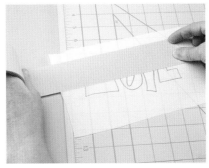

2 Create a single-sided duct tape fabric over the right side of the pencil drawing.

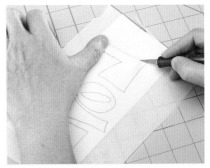

3 Flip the sheet over and cut out the word or design by following the pencil marks (visible through the back of the parchment paper) with a craft knife.

When you're ready to adhere your letters or shapes, simply peel off the parchment paper as if it were a sticker, then place the tape element on your project.

Chapter 2
Fashionable Accessories

With the rising popularity of duct tape, you've probably seen your share of duct tape wallets by now, as well as a purse or two and maybe even a prom dress (I humbly bow to the creators of stunning tape dresses!). But I'm here to let you know that duct tape has *so much* more potential when it comes to making attractive, functional, fashionable accessories that are not only fun to make but also express your unique style.

More colors and patterns of tape are available now than ever, so it's easy to find a flavor that suits you.

In this section I'll show you how to make cute jewelry that will turn heads, wallets that make a statement and purses to complete your favorite outfits perfectly.

Feather Earrings

When you use chrome tape for these earrings, people will have a hard time believing you when you tell them they're made from duct tape! Alternatively, these feathers would look great in just about any color.

MATERIALS LIST

cutting mat

craft knife

duct tape: chrome

shrink plastic

feather template

fine-point permanent marker

parchment paper

heat gun

¹⁄₁₆" (2mm) hole punch

Ranger Vintaj Patina paint for metal

jump rings, 2

earring hooks, 2

needle-nose pliers

Visit **artistsnetwork.com/ducttapediscovery** for more duct tape discoveries.

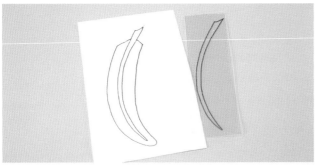

1 Using the Feather Earrings Template, trace the quill part of the feather onto shrink plastic using a fine-point permanent marker. Cut out the quill shape.

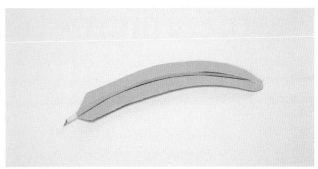

2 Trace the feather shape onto a piece of parchment paper and cover the traced lines with a strip of tape. Cut out the feather shape using a craft knife on a cutting mat, and peel off the parchment. Position the quill down the center of the sticky side of the tape feather shape.

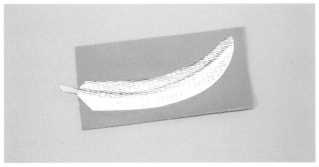

3 Position the feather onto another piece of matching duct tape, sticky sides together.

4 Cut the excess tape around the shape using the craft knife. Create the lines of the feather by cutting through the tape at an angle from the quill to the outside. Keep your cuts parallel and about 1/16" (2mm) apart.

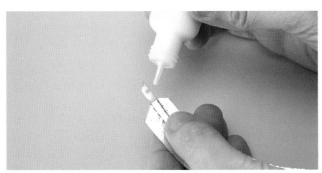

5 Punch a 1/16" (2mm) hole at the end of the quill. Cover the tip of the quill with Ranger Vintaj Patina for metal paint to give the quill a more natural color.

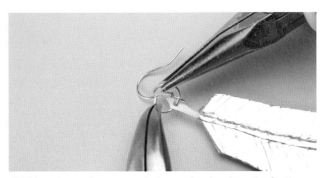

6 Use a jump ring to attach the earring hook to the feather. Repeat steps 1–6 to create the second earring.

Heart Earrings

Shrink plastic used as a filler gives these earring shapes a bit more body and structure than tape alone. I love romantic hearts, but just about any shape is easy to cut from the plastic.

MATERIALS LIST

cutting mat

craft knife

duct tape: tie-dye, chrome

shrink plastic, white or clear

parchment paper

fine-point permanent marker

parchment paper

⅛" (3mm) eyelets, 2

⅛" (3mm) hole punch

eyelet setter

hammer

jump rings, 2

earring hooks, 2

needle-nose pliers

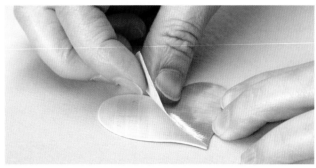

1 Cut a heart shape out of shrink plastic. I used a die-cut shape. Cover it with a strip of tie-dye duct tape, turn the piece over onto a cutting mat and cut around the edge of the shrink plastic to cut out the heart.

Take a second piece of tie-dye duct tape and stick it to a piece of parchment paper. Place the heart, duct tape side down, onto the second piece of tape and trace around the heart with a marker.

2 Using a craft knife on a cutting mat, cut out the second heart.

Peel the parchment paper off the second heart, match up the two shapes and adhere the second heart to the plastic.

3 Punch a ⅛" (3mm) hole at one lobe of the heart. Place an eyelet in the hole.

4 Set the eyelet on the reverse side using an eyelet setter and a hammer. Embellish the heart with a small chrome heart of duct tape.

TIP: Use a toothpick to help place small, sticky pieces.

VARIATION

5 Use a jump ring to attach the earring hook through the eyelet.

Repeat steps 1–5 to create the second earring.

Multicord Cuff

Using a patterned tape for some of the cords in this bracelet adds a lot of interest, even though the pattern itself is not clearly visible. I like just a few cords made from the chrome tape for a bit of pretty sparkle.

MATERIALS LIST

twine or cord (paper cord works well)

cutting mat

craft knife

duct tape: pattern with colors you like, chrome

1/16" (2mm) hole punch

hammer

overall buckle

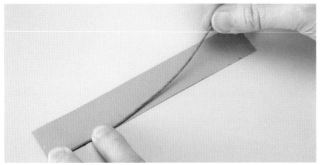

1 To make an 8" (20cm) bracelet (when clasped; adjust accordingly): Cut nine 6" (15cm) strands of twine or cord. Cut five 6" (15cm) lengths of tape, and cut each in half lengthwise to create ten half-widths of tape.

Place one strand of cord on the edge of one piece of tape and roll it up so your cord is covered in tape. Roll the strand back and forth on your worktable several times, as if you are rolling dough for a pretzel, to make sure the tape is adhered well down the entire length of the cord.

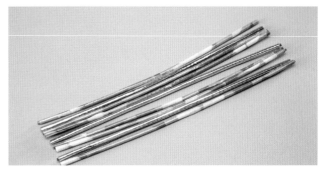

2 Repeat step 1 for all nine strands of cord. I used six strands of metallic butterfly tape and three strands of chrome.

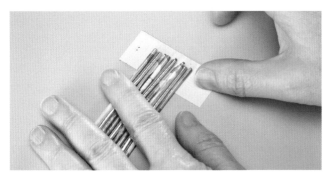

3 Line up the covered strands flush and wrap a piece of tape all the way around them to keep them in place. Repeat at the other end of the strands.

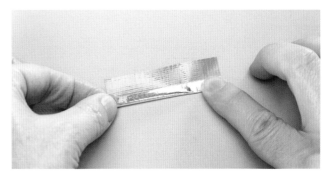

4 Cut a 2½" × 1" (6cm × 2cm) piece of tape and fold it in on itself lengthwise, about ¼"(6mm).

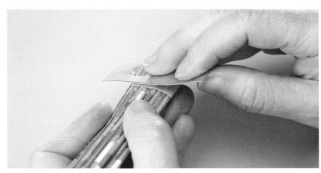

5 Wrap this piece around the wrapped ends with the folded portion at the bottom.

6 Fold a 1¾" × 3½" (4cm × 9cm) piece of tape up and over the folded piece. This will cover the strand ends.

7 Then use a 2½" × 2" (6cm × 5cm) piece of tape as another layer. Notch the corners and fold the flaps around the strands.

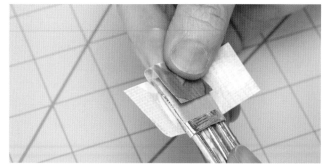

8 Fold the center piece down first, but fold it to itself at the top, about ¼" (6mm), to create a thin "flap" at the top. Then fold the sides in.

9 Punch a hole in the extended tape flap in the center of the width, using a 1/16" (2mm) punch.

10 Push the shank for the button through the hole from the back to the front of the bracelet. Push the button portion down on the pin of the shank, then hammer the button to secure.

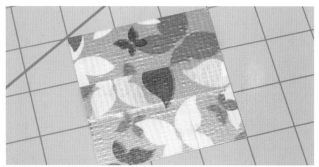

11 Create a single-sided fabric of tape 3" × 3" (8cm × 8cm).

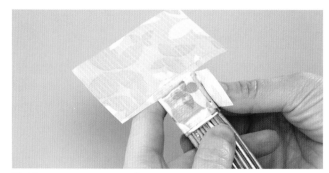

12 Attach this piece of tape at the opposite end of the bracelet in such a way that reveals a bit of the fold of the first wrap. Make slits in the tape at the end of the strands and fold those flaps in to adhere.

Visit artistsnetwork.com/ducttapediscovery for more duct tape discoveries.

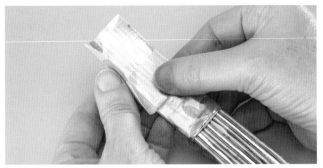

13 Fold the tape above the strands in on itself, in thirds, to create a tape strap for the buckle.

14 Bend the hook of the buckle slightly to mimic the curve of a wrist.

15 Thread the tape strap through the hook and then fold it down over the other side of the buckle.

16 Use a 1" × 1½" (3cm × 4cm) piece of matching tape to secure the strap to the bracelet.

DETAIL

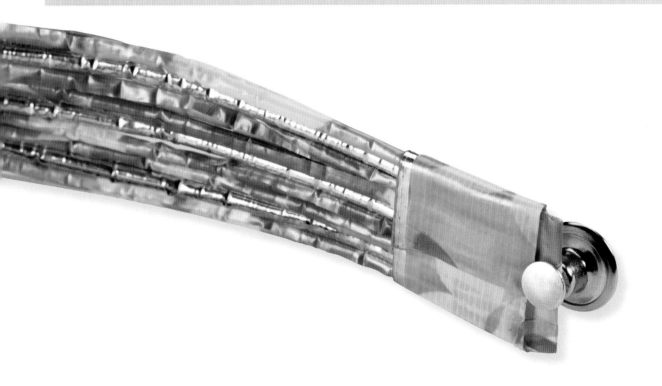

Feather Cuff

Think of this cuff as your canvas. I used a feather as a focal point, but you could just as easily decorate this cuff with a word or other shapes that have personal significance to you.

MATERIALS LIST

cutting mat

craft knife

duct tape: lilac, paisley, teal, white

parchment paper

pencil

heavy-duty snap

hammer

OPEN

Visit **artistsnetwork.com/ducttapediscovery** for more duct tape discoveries.

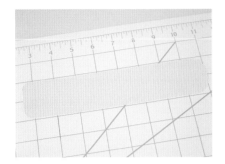

1 Cut a 1⅞" × 8½" (5cm × 22cm) strip of lilac tape. Adjust the length based on the size of your wrist. Round the corners.

2 Cut a 7¼" (18cm) strip of paisley tape. Cut the piece in half length-wise. Place the half-width strips along the edges of the length of the lilac strip.

Peel up the tape and fold the flaps around the back. There should be more tape on the back flaps than on the front.

3 Cut two decorative end pieces out of the paisley tape and attach one at each end of the cuff. The flourished end should be on the front.

4 Round the corners and then make several slits in the tape so it wraps around the back more easily.

5 Wrap the slit pieces around the back.

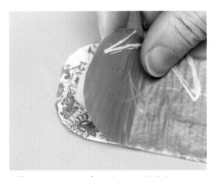

6 Cut a strip of teal tape slightly smaller than the cuff piece, round the corners and adhere it to the back to cover the remaining sticky area.

7 Draw a feather (or use the Feather Cuff Template) on paper. Trace the feather onto parchment paper. Place a piece of tape over the feather shape, turn it over and cut out the feather.

8 Cut a thin strip of white tape for the vein/quill through the middle of the feather. Adhere the feather to the front of the cuff.

9 Attach half of a snap on one end of the cuff. Attach the other half of the snap at the other end of the cuff.

Lifesaver Necklace

These little white circles remind me of the roll of Lifesaver candy my grandmother always had in her purse for me. While you can cut these circles by hand, I highly recommend using a die-cut system, such as the one I used from Spellbinders.

MATERIALS LIST

cutting mat

craft knife

duct tape: lime, pastel blue, teal, white

circle template or die-cut machine

shrink plastic, clear

heat gun

heat-resistant craft mat

1/16" (2mm) hole punch

1/16" (2mm) eyelets, 10

eyelet setter

hammer

jump rings, 6

jeweler's pliers

necklace chain

Visit **artistsnetwork.com/ducttapediscovery** for more duct tape discoveries.

1 From clear shrink plastic, cut five 1" (3cm) circles, each with a ½"(13mm) circle cut from the center.

Use a heat gun to shrink the plastic rings.

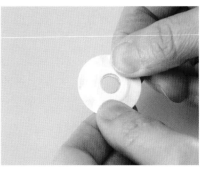

2 Cut two identical duct tape circles ½" (13mm) larger in diameter than the shrunken plastic. Cut holes from the middle that are the same size as the center hole on the shrunken plastic rings.

3 Place the tape circles on each side of the plastic circle and align the edges of the outside and the inner circles as best you can. Use your fingernail to burnish the two sticky sides together. Repeat steps 2 and 3 for each plastic circle.

4 Cut ten ½" (13mm) diameter circles of duct tape in a combination of three colors. Each should have a center hole the same size as the plastic hole. Cut each circle in half.

5 Create combinations of two different colored halves on both sides of the white taped pieces. Use a toothpick for positioning if you're like me and feel your fingers get in the way.

6 Punch a 1/16" (2mm) hole on each side of the circle.

7 Set an eyelet in each hole. Repeat on each circle.

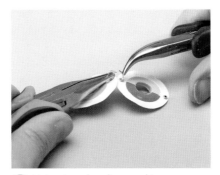

8 Using jewelry pliers and jump rings, connect the circles through the eyelets.

9 Attach the strand of circles to the chain you have chosen to complete the necklace.

TIP: Consider making matching earrings.

Pendant Necklace

The key to this cute necklace is to keep the design simple since the "canvas" size is small. In lieu of a tree, consider a single initial or simple symbol such as a heart or star.

MATERIALS LIST

oval template or die-cut machine

¼" (6mm) hole punch

shrink plastic, black

heat gun

heat-resistant craft mat

wooden rod

cutting mat

craft knife

duct tape: white, black, red

fine file (optional)

needle or toothpick

parchment paper

pencil

jump rings, 2

needle-nose pliers

leather cord or necklace chain

doming resin

VARIATION

Visit **artistsnetwork.com/ducttapediscovery** for more duct tape discoveries.

1 Cut a 2¾" × 3¾" (7cm × 10cm) oval out of shrink plastic. Punch a ¼" (6mm) hole at the top.

2 Shrink the plastic using a heat gun.
 TIP: Hold the end of the oval down with a wooden rod to prevent the plastic from curling in and sticking to itself.

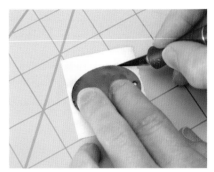

3 Place a piece of white tape on the oval. Flip over the oval and trim the excess tape from around the perimeter using a craft knife.

4 Smooth the edges of the tape around the oval using a file, if you like. Use a needle tool or toothpick to punch through the tape at the spot for the hole.

5 Trace the oval on a piece of parchment paper.

6 Draw a design in the shape.

7 Place a piece of tape over the drawn design. Flip the tape and paper over to cut out the shape using a craft knife.

8 Remove the parchment paper from the tape shapes and carefully place the elements on the oval.

9 Hook a jump ring through the hole and run a necklace or cord through the jump ring.
 TIP: Protect your finished pendant by giving it a coat of a jeweler's grade doming resin such as ICE.

Daisy Necklace

Flowers come in so many shapes and colors, and your options for this necklace are endless. You could even make each flower different for a more eclectic bouquet.

MATERIALS LIST

cutting mat

craft knife

duct tape: hot pink, pastel pink, cream, pastel blue

1/16" (2mm) hole punch

hammer

seed beads, 5

head pins, 5

round-nose pliers

waxed-linen or leather cord

metal cording crimp ends, 2

metal clasp

needle-nose pliers

Visit **artistsnetwork.com/ducttapediscovery** for more duct tape discoveries.

1 Fold three different colored small pieces of duct tape in half. Cut out flower shapes in three different sizes. (I used Spellbinders' flower dies.)

2 Using a fourth color of duct tape, cut out a smaller flower and adhere it to the smallest of the double-sided flowers.

3 Stack the flowers together—largest on the bottom, smallest on the top—and punch a hole through the center of the entire stack.

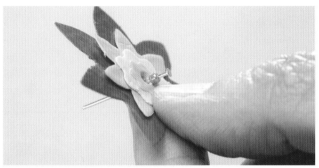 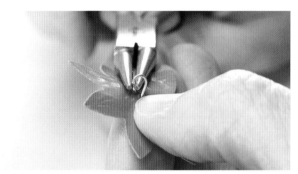

4 Thread a seed bead onto a head pin and stick the pin through the layers of flowers, front to back.

5 Use pliers to create a loop at the end of the head pin. Repeat steps 1–5 four more times to create a total of five identical flowers.

6 String each flower onto a leather or waxed-linen cord.

7 On each end of the cord, use pliers to squeeze on a cording crimp end. Attach a clasp of your choice.

Eye Mask

While this mask is for masquerading, you could leave the mask sans eye holes for the sleeping-beauty variety. Indulge your inner Cat Woman (or Superman). Who says you need to wait for Halloween?

MATERIALS LIST

cutting mat

craft knife

duct tape: black, white

⅛" (3mm) hole punch

⅛" (3mm) eyelets, 2

⅛" (3mm) eyelet setter

hammer

elastic strand

cording crimp ends, 2

jump rings, 2

needle-nose pliers

black marker

Visit **artistsnetwork.com/ducttapediscovery** for more duct tape discoveries.

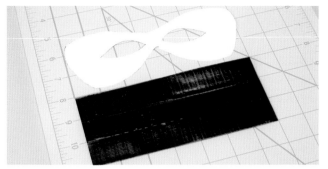

1 Cut out a template for your mask from paper. Create a 3" × 7" (8cm × 18cm) double-sided piece of black duct tape fabric.

2 Use the mask template to cut out the mask shape using scissors or a craft knife.

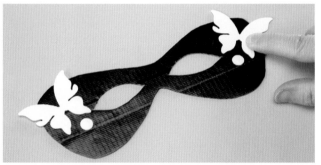

3 Embellish the mask with duct tape stickers as you like. (I used die-cut butterflies.)

TIP: If you have a sticker hanging off the edge of the mask, be sure to cover the back with a matching piece of tape so it doesn't stick to your hair or face. In this case, I matched another butterfly on the back.

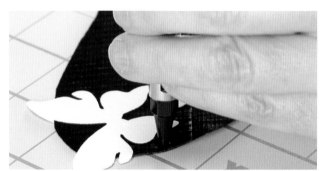

4 Punch a hole at each end of the mask and set an eyelet in each one.

5 Attach a cording crimp to each end of the elastic.

TIP: If your mask is black and the white tape adhesive starts to show, use a black permanent marker to color the adhesive black.

6 Connect the strand to the eyelets using the jump rings.

VARIATION

Use different stickers on the back to make a reversible mask!

Circles Wallet

This wallet comes together in a flash, and since it's meant to hold cards only, it will be ultrathin. Decorations for your wallet may vary, depending on the patterned tape you choose.

MATERIALS LIST

cutting mat

craft knife

straightedge

duct tape: original, metallic circles

parchment paper

circles template or die-cut machine

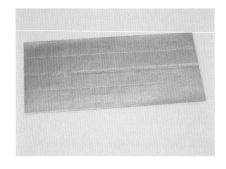

1 Create an 8½" × 4" (22cm × 10cm) double-sided piece of original duct tape fabric.

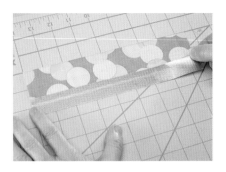

2 Cut three lengths of the patterned tape 8½" (22cm) long. Set two aside on parchment. Cut a half-width of original duct tape 8½" (22cm) long. Adhere it to one side of a circles strip, overlapping the circles strip by ½" (13mm). Repeat for a second strip.

Cut six 3⅞" × 1½" (10cm × 4cm) pieces of original tape and place them on parchment paper.

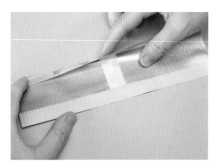

3 Flip over one of the patterned strips that has original tape along the bottom. Place two of the short original strips on the patterned sticky side (leave a gap in the middle). Fold over the excess patterned tape.

Repeat this step for the other patterned strip with original tape at the bottom.

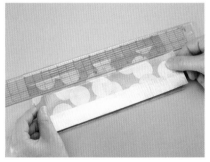

4 Attach the first row of patterned/original tape about ¾" (2cm) from the top of the wallet.

Attach the second row of patterned/original tape about ¾" (2cm) from the first row.

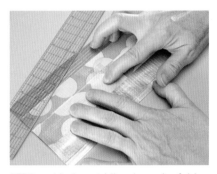

5 Burnish the middle where the fold will be.

6 On the third strip of patterned tape, attach an 8½"-long (22cm) strip of original tape (the full width) and use it to adhere this to the very bottom of the wallet. Wrap the excess around the front.

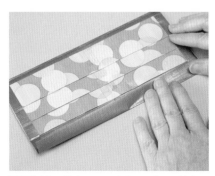

7 Finish off the remaining edges (sides and top) with half-widths of duct tape trimmed to size.

8 Fold the wallet along the seam. Add embellishments on the front of the fold.

TIP: Place the folded wallet under a weight overnight so it will stay closed.

Butterfly Wallet

This divided wallet will keep your presidents nicely aligned on one side and your important notes and receipts on the other. An easy Velcro closure keeps everything tucked safely inside.

MATERIALS LIST

cutting mat

craft knife

straightedge

duct tape: chocolate, pastel blue, teal

parchment paper

pencil

Velcro strips

Visit **artistsnetwork.com/ducttapediscovery** for more duct tape discoveries.

1 Create an 8" × 9" (20cm × 23cm) double-sided piece of duct tape fabric. Round two of the corners on the ends of one 9" (23cm) side.

2 Cut an 8" × 3" (20cm × 8cm) double-sided piece of matching duct tape fabric. This will become a divider in the center of the wallet.

3 Fold the end of the fabric opposite the side with the rounded corners up 3" (8cm), press and unfold. Position the divider piece so the bottom edge is at the fold. Cut an 8" (20cm) strip of half-width tape and use it to adhere the bottom edge of the divider to the wallet.

Flip the divider down and secure it with the second half-width tape strip.

Cut another thin strip of tape and center it over the unfinished top edge of the divider.

4 Fold the bottom half of the wallet up over the divider and press and snuggle it together to make sure it's all aligned nicely.

5 Finish the top edge of the folded portion with another strip of tape. Secure each side of the folded wallet with a strip of tape the height of the folded portion.

6 Cut a 9" (23cm) strip of tape. Adhere it to the front of the flap portion and leave a ½" (13mm) overhang. Round the overhang tape to match the rounded corners of the flap.

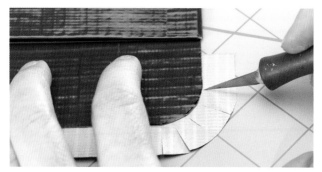

7 Cut slits into the tape around the corners.

8 Fold in the overhang tape. Cut a length of tape just under 8" (20cm) and round the corners. Use this to cover the tape that was folded over on the inside of the flap to make a more finished edge.

9 Use the Butterfly Wallet Grass Template (bottom layer) or sketch your own. Trace it onto parchment paper and cover it with a strip of complementary duct tape.

10 Cut out the grass and carefully adhere the strip to the bottom of the wallet.

11 Cut out unconnected sections of grass from a second color using the Butterfly Wallet Grass Template (top layer) and layer the individual pieces of grass over parts of the first grass strip to create a dimensional effect. Cut out two butterflies of matching colors and adhere them above the grass. (I used a Spellbinders' butterfly die.)

12 Attach Velcro squares to the inside of the flap and the back outside of the wallet.

INSIDE

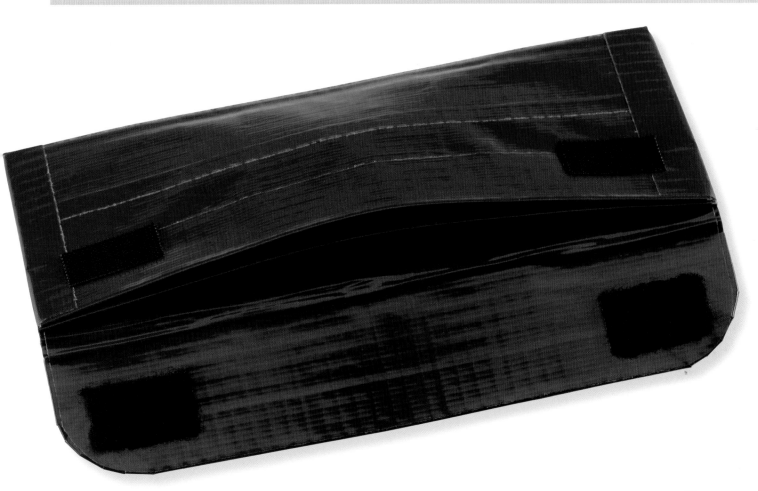

House Wallet

This little wallet is small but mighty. It holds both cards and bills, and the inside is as cute as the outside. A simple house adorns this version, but of course other simple elements would be just as stylish.

MATERIALS LIST

cutting mat

craft knife

straightedge

duct tape: orange, teal, beige, white, green, red

parchment paper

pencil

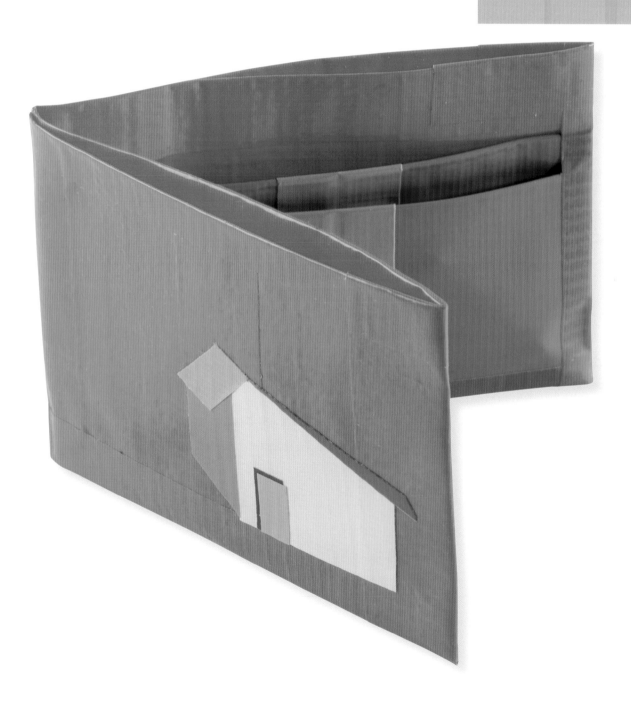

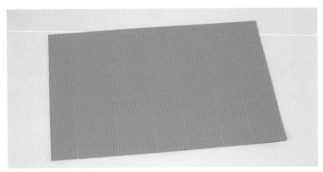

1 Create a 6" × 8½" (15cm × 22cm) double-sided fabric out of orange duct tape.

2 Center two half-widths of tape over the 8½" (22cm) sides to finish them.

3 Fold the fabric in half so the two finished ends meet at the top. This forms the bill-holding pocket. Seal the sides together using orange tape.

Insert a piece of tape inside of both seams as well to seal them.

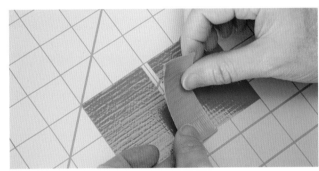

4 Cut eight 2½" (6cm) pieces of teal tape. Cut four 2½" × 1" (6cm × 3cm) pieces of beige tape.

Position two pieces of teal tape on the cutting mat so that two widths of tape span 4" (10cm), and leave a ¼" (6mm) gap.

Center a beige strip over the gap.

5 Keeping the three pieces intact, remove this from the cutting mat and flip it over. Cut a 4" (10cm) fabric length of teal tape. Adhere it to the sticky side of the teal/beige piece. Fold over the excess on top.

Repeat to make three more pockets.

6 Cut an 8½" (22cm) half-width strip of orange tape and use it to adhere the bottom edges of two pockets to the wallet, leaving ½" (13mm) of orange showing at the top of the wallet.

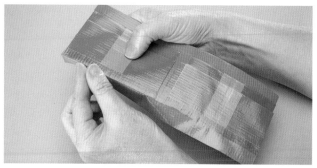

7 Line up the second set of pockets along the bottom of the wallet and attach with a second half-width of orange tape. Wrap the excess orange tape around the bottom fold.

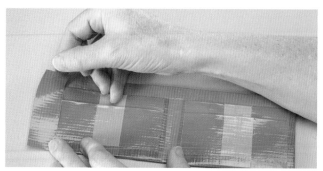

8 Cut a 3" (8cm) length of orange tape in half. Use one piece on each outside edge of the wallet to seal the pocket sides.

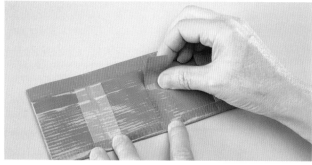

9 Cut a 3" × ¾" (8cm × 2cm) piece of orange tape and run it down the middle of the fold, sealing the inner sides of the pockets.

10 Using the House Wallet Template, trace each piece on a separate portion of parchment paper.

11 Cover each piece with a different color of tape and cut one section out at a time so you have a front that is white, a door that is red, etc.

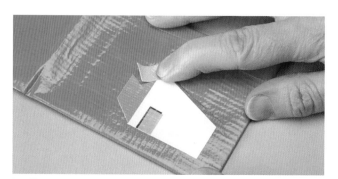

12 Reassemble the pieces on the front of the wallet to create the house.

VARIATION

Contributing artist Caitlin Nance designed this cute Plaid Owl Wallet. I love the hand stitches around the owl.

Visit **artistsnetwork.com/ducttapediscovery** for more duct tape discoveries.

Tote Bag

Duct tape is so strong and durable that it's perfect for carrying whatever you can fit in this bag. Trips to the farmer's market, commuting on the train or visits to the library are about to get a lot more fun!

MATERIALS LIST

cutting mat

craft knife

straightedge

duct tape: original, orange, purple, hot pink, lilac

parchment paper

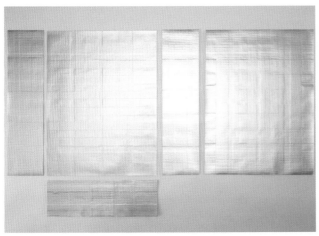

1 Create double-sided fabric for the five panels of the bag. Make two panels for the front and back 12" × 9" (29cm × 23cm). Create two panels for the sides 3" × 12" (8cm × 29cm). Create one panel for the bottom 3" × 9" (8cm × 23cm).

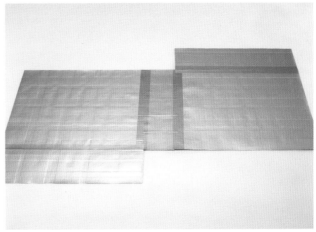

2 Use half-width strips of matching tape to connect the seams. Tape the bottom to the front and back panels first to create one long piece of fabric. Then attach one side panel to the front panel and the other side panel to the opposite side of the back panel.

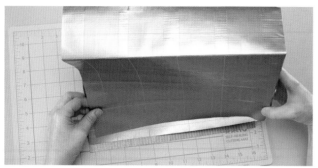

3 Fold the bag up and secure one side panel to the front and the other side panel to the back using half-widths of matching tape that are the same length as the bag.

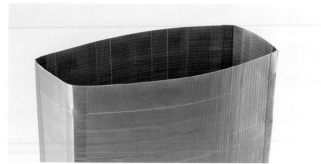

4 Secure the side panels to the bottom panel. Then cut a second set of half-width strips and finish off all the seams on the inside.

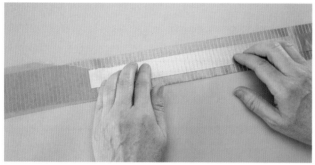

5 To create the straps, cut two strips of duct tape, each 50" (127cm) long. Cut a half-width strip of tape 26" (66cm) long. Place these strips in the very center (both length and width) of the 50" (127cm) strips.

To keep the 50" (127cm) strip from becoming unwieldy and sticking to other things, cover the ends with parchment paper.

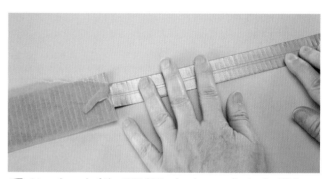

6 At each end of the 26" (66cm) strip, cut slits in the 50" (127cm) piece and fold the flaps onto the 26" (66cm) strip.

7 Working with one end at a time, remove the protective parchment and attach the length of tape to the inside of the bag, 2" (5cm) from each side. Each strip should go to the bottom of the inside of the bag. The folded piece will now be a handle.

Repeat on the opposite side of the bag to create the second handle.

8 Cut a half-width strip of tape equal to the length from one handle on the front to the opposite handle on the back. Place one half of the tape on the outside of the bag, clip the corners and fold the flaps to the inside.

Visit artistsnetwork.com/ducttapediscovery for more duct tape discoveries.

9 Attach another half-width of tape between the straps, on the front and back, to finish off the edge of the bag.

10 Decorate the bag with layers of multisized duct shapes in a variety of colors. Here I used an assortment of Spellbinders dies.

DETAIL

Visit **artistsnetwork.com/ducttapediscovery** for more duct tape discoveries.

Coin Purse

This fun little purse is too cute to keep inside a larger purse. Luckily the wrist strap makes it easy for you to carry it on its own. I used patterned tape for the outside, but a solid tape works just as well.

MATERIALS LIST

cutting mat

craft knife

straightedge

duct tape: floral pattern, pastel pink

self-sealing sandwich bag

⅛" (3mm) hole punch

⅛" (3mm) eyelets, 2

eyelet setter

hammer

jump ring

needle-nose pliers

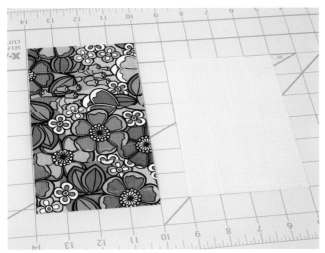

1 Create a 4" × 7¾" (10cm × 20cm) piece of single-sided tape fabric. Create a second sheet of single-sided fabric that's 4" × 6" (10cm × 15cm).

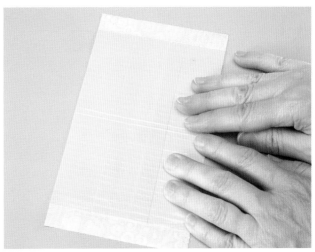

2 Place the small piece in the center of the large piece, sticky sides together, so you have exposed tape at either end.

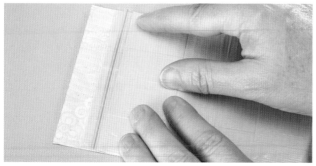

3 Cut the top off a Ziploc bag and trim the zipper to 4" (10cm) long. Separate the zipper. Place half of the zipper at one end and the other half at the other. Secure the bottom edge of the zipper with a piece of matching tape (in this case, pink).

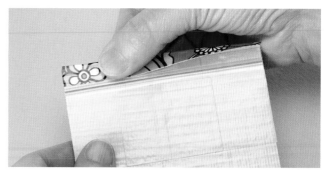

4 Secure the top half of the zipper by folding over the remaining sticky portion of the outside fabric.

5 Fold the piece together and seal the zipper shut. Burnish the bottom fold. Cut a length of tape (that matches the outside) the height of the coin purse. Cut the tape in half lengthwise to create two half-widths. Bind the sides together using the strips.

6 To create the wrist strap, cut a strip of the inside color tape to 10" × 1½" (25cm × 4cm). Fold the length in on itself almost into thirds.

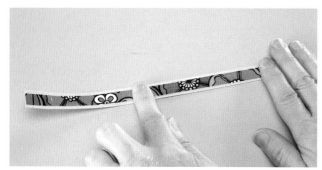

7 Cover the seam where the tape meets with a ⅜" × 10" (1cm × 25cm) strip of tape that matches the outside of the bag. Trim the ends to a slight taper.

8 Fold the strip in half and wrap a 1¾" (4cm) piece of tape around the bottom. Be sure to leave about ½" (13mm) hanging off the end to add an eyelet.

TIP: Trim small triangles where the folds will be to keep the tape from bulking up.

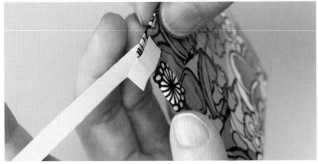

9 Create a tab at the top of the coin purse by wrapping a ⅜" × 9" (1cm × 23cm) strip of tape around the top edge of the purse. Pinch 1" (3cm) of the tape together at one corner to create a tab that is ½" (13mm) long.

10 Punch a hole in the tab and at the end of the wrist wrap.

11 Set an eyelet in each hole.

12 Link the eyelets together using a jump ring.

Ovals Purse

When you see how easy this purse comes together, you're going to want to make one to match each of your favorite outfits. Decorate the bag with whatever shapes suit your style.

MATERIALS LIST

cutting mat

craft knife

straightedge

duct tape: beige, pastel blue, chocolate

Ziploc press and seal bag, quart or gallon size

¼ " (6mm) hole punch

¼ " (6mm) eyelets, 2

eyelet setter

hammer

swivel hooks, 2

parchment paper

oval template or die-cut machine

flexible plastic

metal swivel hook clasps, 2

Visit **artistsnetwork.com/ducttapediscovery** for more duct tape discoveries.

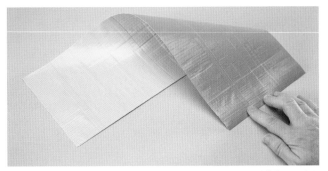

1 Create a 6" × 17½" (15cm × 44cm) double-sided fabric. This one is beige on one side and blue on the other.

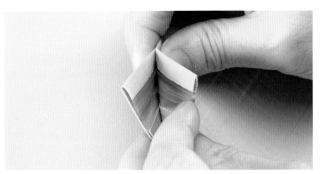

2 Cut the zipper part off the Ziploc bag and trim to the width of your fabric. Separate the zipper into two separate pieces, and position one half of it along one 6" (15cm) end. Cut a half-width of beige tape 6" (15cm) long and use it to secure the zipper piece to the beige side of the fabric.

Repeat on the other half of the zipper at the opposite end of the beige side of the fabric.

3 Cut a 6" (15cm) length of pastel blue duct tape and use it to secure the top portion of each zipper. The excess duct tape will fold over the top portion of the bag to the outside.

4 Match up the zipper halves and seal them together.

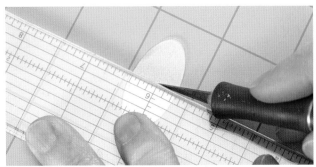

5 Cut two lengths of pastel blue tape the same length as the folded bag. Wrap a piece of tape around each side of the bag to seal it.

6 Using an oval template, cut two ovals out of flexible plastic (e.g., shrink plastic or recycled packaging). Cut the ovals in half.

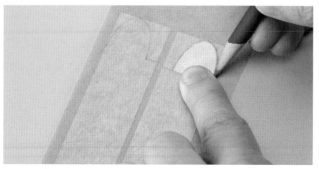

7 Cut four half-width strips of duct tape the length of the bag plus half the oval shape. Place the half of the oval at the top of the strip flush to one edge. Trace it and cut off the excess tape.

8 Adhere the strips to the outer edges of the front and back of the bag with the oval tips hanging off the top. Attach each plastic half oval to the matching part of the tape.

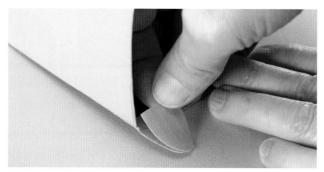

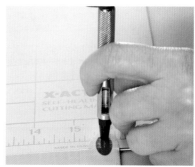

9 Cover the half oval with a piece of matching tape. (Place a piece of tape on parchment, draw the shape onto the parchment using the oval template and cut out the tape oval.)

10 Place a smaller decorative oval on the outside of each tab. Punch a hole through each oval tab.

11 Set an eyelet in each hole with the fronts of the eyelets on the outside of the bag.

12 Using the Ovals Purse Tapered Strap Template, layer strips of duct tape to the length of the strap you want. Feel free to use one color on one side and another color on the other. Trim each end to a slight taper.

Cut thin strips of tape in a matching color to wrap around the edges of the strap. Doing so ensures the two layers of tape don't separate and creates a fashionable strip of color on one side.

13 Thread a clasp onto the bottom of the strap and fold it up. Set an eyelet to secure the clasp in a loop.

14 Wrap a strip of tape around the edge of the folded piece to mask it. Repeat steps 13 and 14 at the other end of the strap.

15 Cut a variety of ovals in different sizes and complementary colors. A die-cut system makes this super easy. Adhere them as you desire on the front of the bag.

DETAIL

Chapter 3
Cards and Gifts

Many of us swoon over pretty stationery, and we're often inspired to create our own heartfelt cards because we know how much they're appreciated by those with whom we share our creations. A handmade greeting creates a connection that just isn't felt over a smartphone or computer monitor.

Duct tape is a great material to use for your handmade greetings, and I think one reason is that it's simply unexpected. And just as paper comes in many pretty colors and patterns, so does tape, so it's easy to create the perfect message you want to send.

Most of the projects in this section combine paper with duct tape because the paper makes the projects easier to fold (and write on). Once you see how easy it is to use tape to express yourself, you'll never worry about a last-minute card for someone again. There's even a postcard that can go through the mail, as well as a cute gift box that no wrapping paper can compete with.

Postcard

Who doesn't like to get things in the mail? In this era of digital communication, a creation such as this is more meaningful than ever before. Use a permanent marker to write the recipient's address and your message.

MATERIALS LIST

cutting mat

craft knife

straightedge

duct tape: white, black, red, teal, lace pattern

parchment paper

pencil

permanent marker (for writing message/address on card)

1 Start with a 5" × 7" (13cm × 18cm) piece of single-sided fabric. Cut a ½" (13mm) notch out of each corner.

2 Gently peel the fabric off your cutting mat and fold the flaps resulting from the notches, onto the sticky side of the tape.

3 Create a 3⅞" × 5⅞" (10cm × 14cm) single-sided fabric. Carefully place this onto the sticky side of the larger piece and cover the folded flaps.

4 Using parchment paper to draw your elements and cut them out, decorate the front of the card with a fun scene. I created a house on a hillside using a Spellbinders die for the houses, but you could do the same by cutting simple squares and triangles.

5 Flip the card over and add a box for a stamp and lines for the address by cutting thin strips of black tape.

Love Note

I could share some bad poetry here to get your love note started, but I'll leave the note writing to you. Whether you make this super-easy note for a friend or a secret crush, your recipient will be duly wowed.

MATERIALS LIST

cutting mat

craft knife

straightedge

duct tape: beige, red, lace pattern, text-message pattern

paper

pencil

bone folder

parchment paper

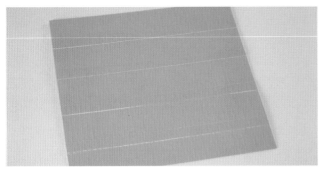

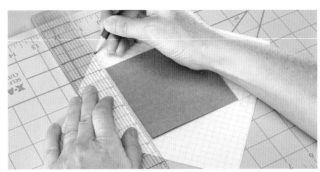

1 Create a sheet of duct tape fabric 7" (18cm) square. Create the fabric directly on paper so you can eventually write a note on the inside. I used graph paper.

2 Create a 4" (10cm) square of paper and center it at a diagonal on the paper side of the fabric. With a straight-edge and pencil, rule lines from one edge of the paper to the other on all four sides.

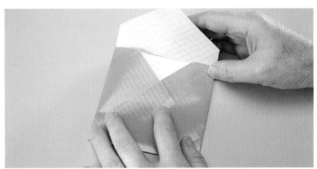

3 Cut out the *V* notches where the lines cross.

4 Using a straightedge and bone folder, score the lines and fold them in toward the center.

5 Embellish the front in a tic-tac-toe style.

6 Write your love note on the paper inside. Seal the note with a duct tape heart or two.

Greeting Card with Envelope

It takes only a few minutes to brighten someone's day. The message you create can be simple, but the expansion of the recipient's heart will be vast. On a smaller scale, this card would be a perfect gift-tag card.

MATERIALS LIST

cutting mat

craft knife

straightedge

duct tape: original, pastel blue, orange

parchment paper

pencil

VARIATION

Ken Oliver used nifty Spellbinders dies to create this lovely card and coordinating envelope.

1 Cut a piece of paper to 11" × 3¾" (28cm × 10cm). Cut a 45-degree "arrow" point at one end and round the tip. (This will be the envelope flap.)

Create a single-sided sheet of original duct tape fabric that is slightly larger than the paper piece. Stick the paper to the duct tape fabric and then use a craft knife to trim off the excess tape around the paper.

2 Fold the straight edge up 4¼" (11cm) and burnish the fold. Wrap 4¼" (11cm) length half-widths of tape around the sides to seal them. This will be the envelope.

3 Sketch a greeting on a piece of parchment paper. The greeting should fit on the front of a 3½" × 4" (9cm × 10cm) card.

4 Cover your letters with a piece of tape. Cut out the greeting from the back using a craft knife.

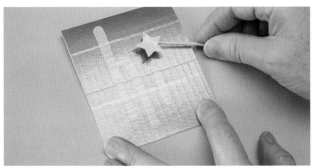

5 Create a card the same way you created the envelope, using a 3½" × 8" (9cm × 20cm) piece of paper, covered in tape and folded with the excess tape trimmed off.

Attach the greeting to the front of the folded card. Add any other embellishments you'd like.

6 Write a message on the paper inside the card and place it in the envelope. Seal the envelope with a duct tape element to complement your card.

Masu Boxes

No more searching for cute little gift boxes to complete that perfect gift for a friend. These boxes come together in mere minutes, and you can use tape colors to complement your gift.

MATERIALS LIST

cutting mat

craft knife

straightedge

duct tape: metallic pink, blue tie-dye, hot pink

paper

parchment paper

1 Create two perfect squares of fabric—paper on one side, duct tape on the other—with one sheet of fabric ½" (13mm) smaller than the other.

Fold the smaller fabric in half. Open the fabric and fold it in half the other direction.

2 Fold one corner to the next. Open the fabric and fold in the opposite direction.

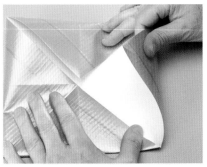

3 Open the fabric and fold each corner to the center point of the fabric.

4 Open two flaps.

5 Fold two flat sides into the center. Open it up and repeat with the other two corners.

6 At the *V*, fold the points backward to create a rectangle.

7 Fold each of the four corners in.

8 Spread the center apart and bring one side up to form the box side.

9 Bring the flap point down into the box. Repeat for the other side. Burnish each edge so the folds stay.

10 Repeat steps 1–9 on the other sheet of fabric to create the lid. Add embellishments to the lid of the box as desired.

Chapter 4
Around the House

If you love DIY home décor, you're going to love making functional and pretty things for your home from duct tape. As I've stated several times already, duct tape comes in colors and patterns to reflect just about anyone's personal taste, but that's not all. Duct tape is durable, so it can stand up to a decent amount of everyday use.

In this section you'll find cool coasters for your next outdoor party or game day get-together, a couple of frames that would work well for mirrors or photos, a gorgeous candle mat—perfect as a table centerpiece—and more. There's even a duct tape mug rug to bring a smile to each morning's cup of joe.

Your next hostess gift is going to be a snap—and who says you can't be the next hostess?

Stemware Tags

No more fumbling, trying to secure those little charm stem tags around your guests' wineglass stems. These fun rings slip on with your eyes closed. Create them to match some coasters, your kitchen or a festive party theme.

MATERIALS LIST

cutting mat

craft knife

straightedge

duct tape: floral pattern, orange

circle template (or die-cut machine)

pen

Visit **artistsnetwork.com/ducttapediscovery** for more duct tape discoveries.

1 Create a double-sided piece of duct tape fabric and trace a circle onto it—about 2½" (6cm) in diameter. Also trace a smaller circle in the center—about ¾" (2cm).

2 Cut out the circles and remove the center. (This is made super easy using two Spellbinders dies simultaneously.)

3 Cut out a decorative round shape in a complementary color that will fit on the cutout shape. Adhere the decorative shape.

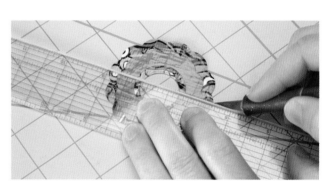

4 Cut one slit through the ring, from the center to the outside, so it will slide on and off a glass stem.

VARIATION

Adorn each tag with a different color tape so your guests can tell their glass apart from the others. Ken Oliver created these stem tags in his own fun style.

Round Coasters and Holder

These coasters and the coaster holder are round, but if cutting circles by hand makes you crazy, the same concept would work just as well using a square or any other shape. I feel a cold drink coming on . . .

MATERIALS LIST

stiffened felt or fun foam

duct tape: orange, pastel blue, hot pink, floral pattern

craft knife

cutting mat

circle stencils (or dies)

parchment paper

pen

Visit **artistsnetwork.com/ducttapediscovery** for more duct tape discoveries.

ROUND COASTERS

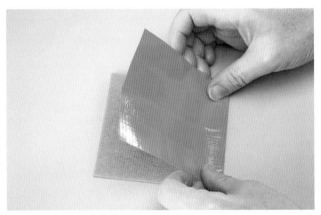

1 Cut a piece of stiffened felt or fun foam and place it on a single-sided sheet of duct tape fabric.

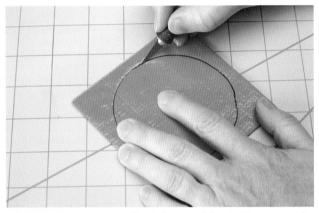

2 Trace a large circle on the felt and cut it out. (Or use a circle die and die-cut machine.)

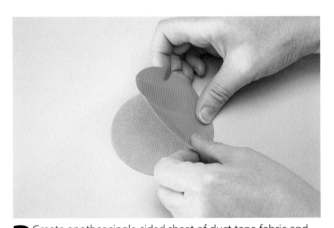

3 Create another single-sided sheet of duct tape fabric and trace the same circle on it.

Cut out the circle and place it on the other side of the exposed felt.

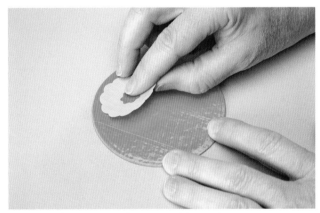

4 Press the tape together around the perimeter. Embellish one side as the top.

COASTER HOLDER

5 Cut a felt circle that is slightly larger than the size of your coasters. Cover one side in duct tape. Cut two more circles of single-sided duct tape of the same size as the felt piece. Place them on parchment paper and set them aside.

Measure a length of stiffened felt by wrapping it around the felt circle and having it overlap a bit.

6 Cut a length of duct tape that matches the length of the felt strip and is twice as wide plus ¼" (6mm). Wrap the tape around the felt strip taking care to leave ¼" (6mm) overhang of tape exposed.

TIP: Temporarily cover the ¼" (6mm) of exposed tape with parchment paper as you cover the felt.

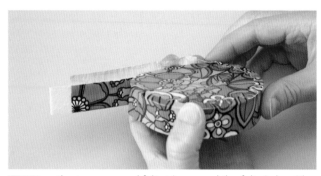

7 Wrap the tape-covered felt strip around the felt circle with the exposed sticky strip meeting the bottom of the holder. Fold the sticky strip onto the bottom circle.

8 Trim any excess felt from the end of the strip and join the ends of the strip with a small piece of matching tape.

9 Remove one of the tape circles from the parchment paper and place it in the center over the exposed felt. Flip over the holder and place the last tape circle on the bottom of the holder to cover the seams.

Visit **artistsnetwork.com/ducttapediscovery** for more duct tape discoveries.

VARIATIONS

This set of coasters by Ken Oliver actually inspired the set I created. I love his offset design elements.

In this variation, padded shipping material replaces the felt for a "fluffier" result.

Mug Rug

Mug rugs are traditionally made from quilted fabric, but I knew it would be fun to create them in duct tape. Paper weaving is something I find relaxing, and I knew that it, too, would be fun with tape.

MATERIALS LIST

duct tape: sweet treats pattern, hot lips pattern, purple, lilac

craft knife

cutting mat

straightedge (with rule lines)

Visit **artistsnetwork.com/ducttapediscovery** for more duct tape discoveries.

1 Cut two 6" (15cm) pieces of tape using complementary patterned tape. Fold each piece in half to create a 3" (8cm) double-sided fabric strip.

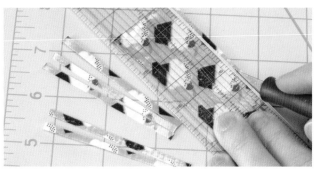

2 Cut one of the 3" (8cm) strips into individual ⅛"-wide (3mm) strips. This is easily done with a C-Thru gridded ruler.

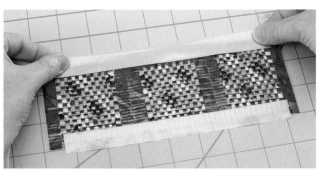

3 Cut ⅛" (3mm) wide slits into the other 3" (8cm) strip. Leave ½" (13mm) uncut at both ends.

4 Weave the individual strips into the slits. Keep the strips in place by sealing the ends with matching tape.
    Repeat steps 1–4 twice, for a total of three mini quilts.

5 Cut a 7½" (19cm) strip of lilac tape and split it lengthwise. Line up the quilts and connect them with these strips.

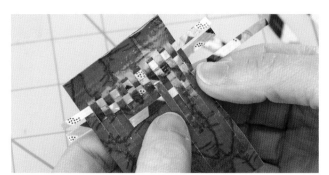

6 Cut a 3⅜" (9cm) strip of lilac tape and split it lengthwise. Adhere it along the ends of the quilt block.
    Cut two ⅞" × 3⅜" (22mm × 9cm) strips of purple tape and cover the seams where the quilts meet.

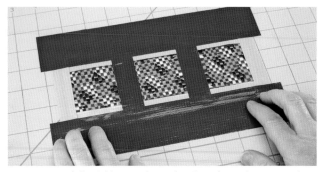

7 Cut two full-width 9½" (24cm) strips of purple tape and set them slightly above and below the lilac strips.

8 Cut a 6½" (17cm) strip of purple tape, split it in half and use it to cover the ends. Allow ½" (13mm) of lilac to show through.

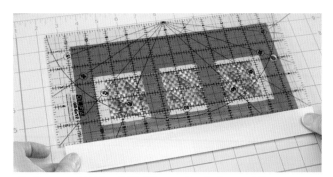

9 Cut two 11½" × 1¼" (29cm × 3cm) pieces of lilac tape. Then cut a 6⅜" (16cm) piece of lilac tape and cut it in half. Place the long strips lengthwise on the mat. Allow ¾" (19mm) of the purple to still show through. Place the short strips along the short sides of the mat and allow ⅛" (3mm) of the purple to still show through.

10 Peel up the mat and flip it over so the sticky side is face up. Create a sheet of purple tape fabric on the exposed adhesive.

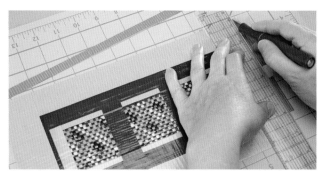

11 Trim off the excess around the edges using a straight-edge and a craft knife.

12 Cut two 11½" (29cm) pieces of hot lips patterned tape and two 7⅜" (19cm) pieces. Fold ¼" (6mm) of the tape onto itself on each of the long strips (not shown).
On the short strips, cut a notch ½" (13mm) from each end and fold the inner flap down.

13 Cut off the notch tab.

14 Attach the long strips on the long sides of the mat and fold the excess over the back. The folded part of the tape should be on the front of the mat. ½"(13mm) of the lilac should be showing.

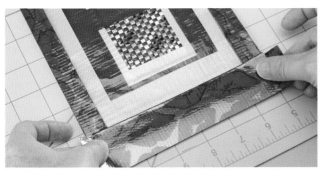

15 Repeat on the shorter sides with the shorter strips. Leave 1⅜" (3cm) of the lilac tape showing.

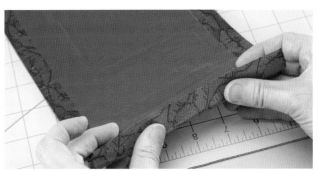

16 Wrap the extended tape on the ends around to the back.

To-Do List (Dry-Erase Board)

Duct tape's slick surface makes it perfect for dry-erase markers. One word of advice: Try to create a writing area that does not include a seam of tape because the marker won't come off the edge of the adhesive well.

MATERIALS LIST

- cardboard
- craft knife
- duct tape: text message pattern, white, red, black
- cutting mat
- magnet
- letter stencils
- parchment paper
- pencil
- dry-erase marker

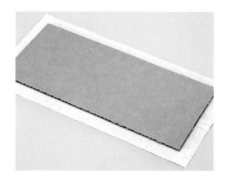

1 Cut a piece of cardboard to the size of the list you want. Cut a piece of duct tape fabric ½" (13mm) larger on each side than the cardboard. Attach the fabric to one side of the cardboard.

Visit artistsnetwork.com/ducttapediscovery for more duct tape discoveries.

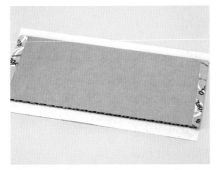

2 Notch the corners to create a flap on each side. Fold the flaps onto the cardboard.

3 Place a layer of fabric, slightly smaller than the whole piece, on the back to completely cover the cardboard. Place a magnet on the back to hang it in your locker or on your refrigerator.

4 Using whatever font you want, trace letters on parchment paper to title your list.

   TIP: Consider phrases like "To Do" or "Need This."

5 Place a piece of cut tape on top of the tracing. Turn it over so the parchment side is up and cut out the letters.

6 Cut out two oval shapes from duct tape in complementary colors. Place one slightly off center of the other to create a shadow effect. Attach it to the top of the main piece. Fold the top part over the cardboard.

7 Cut a strip of white duct tape the length of the remaining cardboard (from under the ovals to the bottom). Attach it to your piece. Peel the bottom of the ovals up slightly to layer your "dry-erase board" tape underneath.

8 Remove the parchment from the back of the cutout letters and adhere them to the oval to finish your dry-erase board.

VARIATION

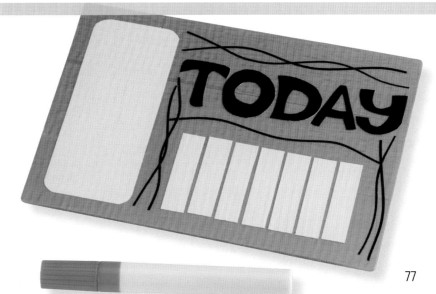

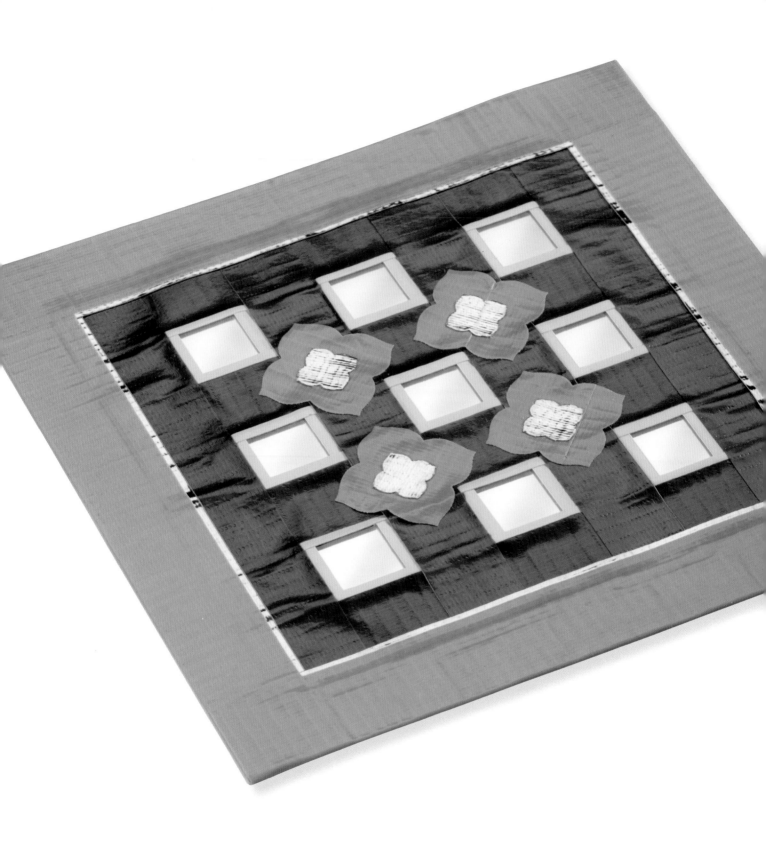

Visit **artistsnetwork.com/ducttapediscovery** for more duct tape discoveries.

Candle Mat

Who says duct tape can't look sophisticated? This pretty mat is as elegant as it is easy to create, and it can save you a trip to the trendy home décor store. I may need to learn to make candles next . . .

MATERIALS LIST

craft knife

cutting mat

duct tape: original, white, lilac, chrome

1" (3cm) mirror squares, 9

parchment paper

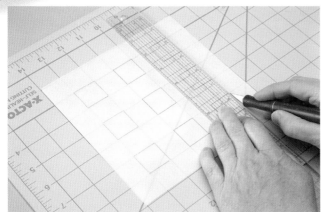

1 Cut a piece of parchment paper to 7" (18cm) square. Then take that paper and cut out evenly spaced squares the size of your mirror pieces. (Tracing the mirrors works well.)

2 Place the parchment template on the sticky side of a 7" (18cm) square piece of single-sided duct tape fabric. (I used white.)

Place the mirrors face up in the cutout squares and press them into the tape adhesive.

3 Remove the parchment paper from the tape.

4 Cut eight 7¼" × 1¼" (18cm × 3cm) strips of matching duct tape. Place the strips between the rows of mirrors and overlap the mirrors by ⅛" (3mm) to keep them in place. Four of the strips will go around the perimeter of the mat.

5 Cut eight 7¼" × 1" (18cm × 3cm) strips of tape in a complementary color. (I used original duct tape.) Center these strips between the mirrors while allowing some of the white to remain visible. Again, four of the strips will go around the perimeter of the mat.

6 Cut four 9½" (24cm) strips of chrome duct tape. Place these strips around the perimeter of the mat. Leave ¾" (19mm) of the original tape visible.

Visit **artistsnetwork.com/ducttapediscovery** for more duct tape discoveries.

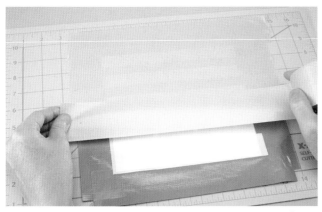

7 Carefully remove the mat from the cutting board and flip it over. Create a layer of lilac tape on the back to cover the adhesive. Don't worry about matching the edges perfectly; you'll trim them later.

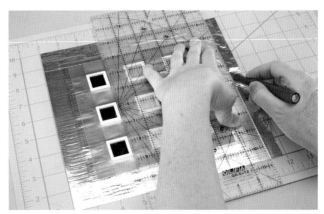

8 Flip the mat back over and trim to leave 1¼" (3cm) of the chrome on each side.

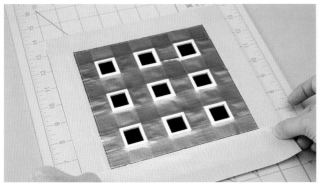

9 Cut four 9" (23cm) strips of lilac tape. Place each strip on the chrome perimeter with ⅛" (3mm) of the tape showing.

Wrap the excess lilac tape around the back to seal the edges.

10 Add duct tape embellishments between the mirrors as desired.

Mosaic Frame

Guests in your home will have to look twice at this frame to realize the tiles are duct tape. Using chrome tape gives the effect of mirrored tiles, and using tie-dye patterned tape resembles dichroic glass. Cool, eh?

MATERIALS LIST

frame, glass and backing taken apart

duct tape: white, chrome, tie-dye patterned

craft knife

cutting mat

gridded straightedge

parchment paper

toothpick

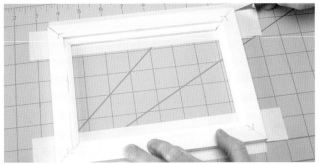

1 Place a piece of white duct tape on the two longest sides of the front of a frame. Each piece should be 2" (5cm) longer than the actual frame.

Flip the frame over and notch out the corners for easy folding.

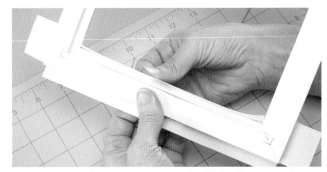

2 Cut slits at the inside corners and fold the flaps over the lip of the frame.

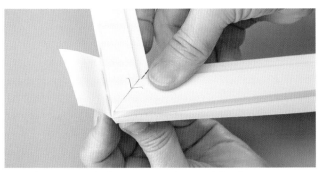

3 Fold the outside flaps onto and around the frame.

TIP: If you get an air bubble in your tape, cut a tiny slit into it using a craft knife and press the tape down.

4 Measure the length of the inside width of the frame and cut two pieces of white duct tape. Adhere those to the shorter sides of the frame and wrap the excess around the edges.

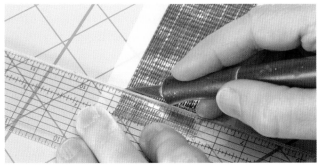

5 Place a strip of tape on parchment paper and use a gridded ruler with a craft knife to cut evenly sized squares. This will create small tiles of duct tape. Repeat this with tape of another color.

I created ¼" (6mm) squares, but you can adjust the size of your tile squares to fit the frame you have (or how much time you have).

6 Carefully place the squares on the frame. They should be evenly spaced but not touching. Using a toothpick will help with this.

Gradually change the color of tape, as shown on the completed frame.

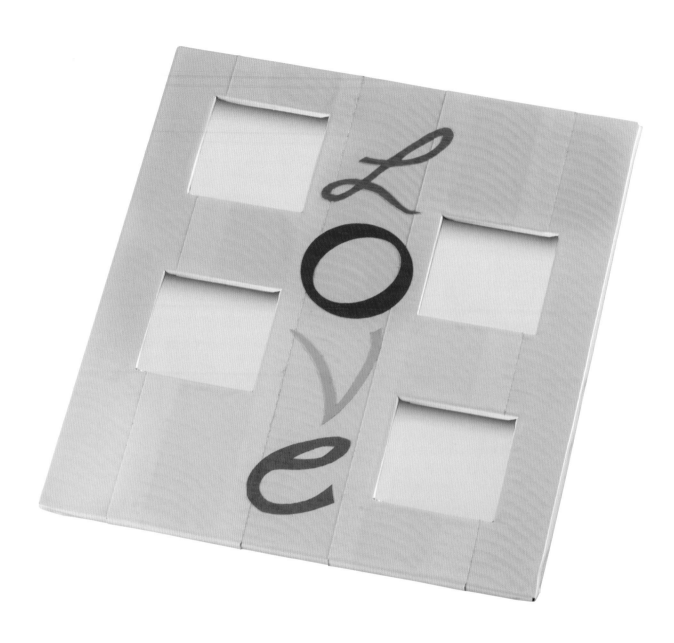

Love Frame

You could easily swap the mirrors in this project with photos of you and a loved one. Feel free to adjust the window openings to accommodate your photos. Whether you go with mirror or pics, remember to look at yourself with love.

MATERIALS LIST

paper

pencil

parchment paper

Love Frame Template

cardboard, 2 pieces

duct tape: white, orange, lime green, hot pink, teal or purple

craft knife

cutting mat

craft glue

1" (3cm) mirror squares, 4

sawtooth hanger

hot glue

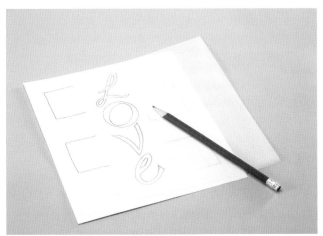

1 Draw your own letters or use the Love Frame Template on paper. Trace the design on parchment paper using a pencil.

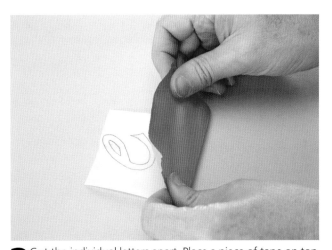

2 Cut the individual letters apart. Place a piece of tape on top of each.

Cut out each letter from the parchment side and set the letters aside.

3 Cut a piece of corrugated cardboard to the same size as your template. Draw the paper's same stenciled squares on the *back* of the cardboard and cut out those areas.

4 Take a second piece of cardboard that is the same size and place it under the first. Trace inside the cutouts.

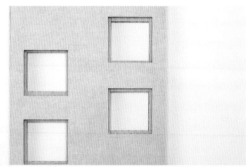

5 Measure lines ⅛" (3mm) outside each square and cut out around the larger square. This will make a lip or shelf for the mirrors to rest on.

6 Cut out a single-sided piece of duct tape fabric that is 1" (3cm) larger on each side than the cardboard frame. Place the top piece of cardboard (the one with smaller holes) face down on the sticky side of the tape.

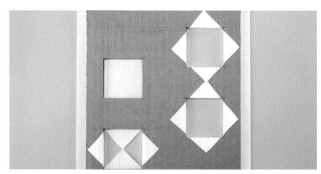

7 Notch the outside corners of the duct tape so you can fold the flaps onto the cardboard later. Using a craft knife, cut an *X* through the tape in each square. Fold the tape flaps onto the back of the cardboard.

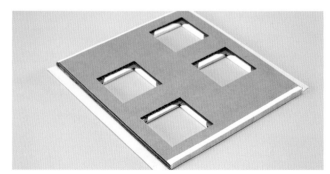

8 Use craft glue to adhere the second piece of cardboard on top of the first. Fold the outside flaps of tape around both pieces.

9 Place the mirrors face down inside the squares. Create a piece of duct tape fabric that is slightly smaller than the overall size of the frame. Place it on the back of the frame and secure the mirrors in place. Burnish the tape to remove any air bubbles.

 TIP: You can use photos or drawings, anything that is the size of the squares you created, in place of the mirrors.

10 Embellish the front of the frame with the *L-O-V-E* letters you cut earlier.

 TIP: If the edges of your adhesives get gummy and dirty, use a rubber eraser to remove it.

 TIP: Use hot glue to glue a sawtooth hanger on the top of the back so you can hang the frame on the wall.

VARIATION

If for a rose
a kiss you'd give
with promises of more
I'd spend the day
from dusk
'til dawn
by picking buds galore

But if there ever
came a day
my garden
had grown bare
a broken heart
would then be mine
and grief beyond compare

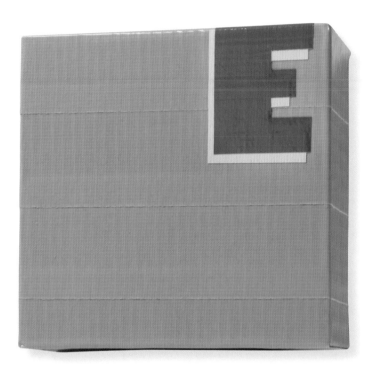

Visit **artistsnetwork.com/ducttapediscovery** for more duct tape discoveries.

Wall Cube Art

Turn those cardboard moving boxes into art for your new walls! It's easy to make these blocks of fun color, and they look great in a group. I created four, but don't stop there if you're inspired!

MATERIALS LIST

cutting mat

craft knife

straightedge

duct tape: teal, white, pastel blue, magenta

parchment paper

cardboard

craft glue

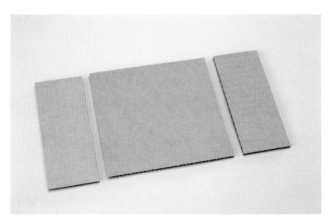

1 To create the box, cut a square piece of cardboard (front), then cut two pieces of cardboard 2" (5cm) wide and the same length as the square piece (sides).

2 Cut two more pieces of cardboard 2" (5cm) wide and about ¼" (6mm) shorter than the side pieces (or the length of the square, minus the two thicknesses of the first strips).

3 Glue the rectangles together to form your box. Start with the two longer pieces, then sandwich in the shorter ones. Wipe away any excess glue.

TIP: You may need to trim the shorter side pieces to make them fit.

4 Create a single-sided sheet of duct tape fabric that will be large enough to cover the front and sides of the box. The width of the box plus 5" (13cm) should be fine.

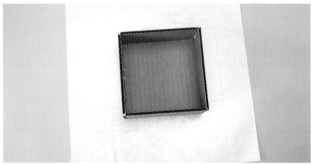

5 Place the box face down in the center of the sticky side of the fabric. Press the center into the tape.

6 Trim the corners of the tape to make wrapping the corners of the box easier.

TIP: Leave the edges of two opposing flaps longer to wrap around the corners.

7 Fold the two longer flaps up and stick them to the box. Wrap the excess around the corners.

8 Trim the excess at the top of the corners and fold the remaining tape into the inside of the box.

Visit **artistsnetwork.com/ducttapediscovery** for more duct tape discoveries.

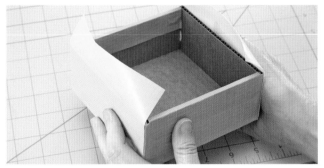

9 Fold the other two flaps up. Trim a small amount off the sides so you can fold the flaps into the inside of the box.

10 Trace a letter (or design element of your choice) onto parchment paper and cover it with a piece of tape.

11 Cut the letter out using a craft knife and remove the parchment.

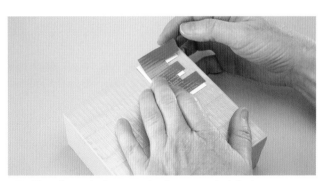

12 Adhere the letter to the front panel of the box. Repeat steps 1–12 to create three more boxes (each with different design elements) for a total of four.

DETAIL

STACY RAUSCH

Duck Does van Doesburg

16" × 20" (41cm × 51cm)
Duct tape on stretched canvas

I created this piece of art for a show at the Del Ray Artisans Gallery in Alexandria, Virginia, for their April 2013 show called "Turn on Your Masters." This piece was my homage to the style of artist Theo van Doesburg. I wanted to put a spin on his style using a nontraditional material to "paint" on the canvas.

MATERIALS LIST

cutting mat

craft knife or rotary cutter

straighedge

duct tape, white, gray, black, blue, yellow, red

stretched canvas

1 Put long strips of duct tape on the cutting mat following the grid lines.

2 Using the straightedge and rotary cutter, cut thin and thick strips and other desired shapes of duct tape from the pieces of tape on the mat.

3 Put the cut pieces of tape on the canvas in your desired pattern. Press firmly. Try to mimic a favorite artist's work or motif, if desired.

TIP: You will need patience to line up the cut pieces of tape on the canvas. Don't worry. Just work slowly and you will be fine!

JOY TIBBETTS

The Leap

9" × 7" (23cm × 18cm)
3-D duct tape art on canvas board

I have loved whales since I was a child. They are majestic and powerful creatures, yet they also seem to have a calming peacefulness about them. This 3-D piece can be displayed on a shelf or mantle, or you can attach a hook to the back and hang this scene in any room to add a splash of art to your walls.

MATERIALS LIST

duct tape: black, white, blue, tie-dye

canvas board 9" × 7" (23cm x 18cm)

cardboard (a cereal box will do)

cutting mat

craft knife

scissors

1 Cover the top three-quarters of your canvas board with the tie-dye duct tape.

2 Use your cutting mat and knife to cut out the portion of the whale that will be stuck directly to the canvas board. Place the black part of the body first, then the white, and then the left fin, top fin and left half of the bottom fin.

3 Create several strips of double-sided duct tape fabric using white and blue tape. Allow 3/8" (9mm) of the adhesive to remain uncovered on both sides. Cut the strips into waves.

4 Using the 3/8" (9mm) of adhesive, attach the first set of waves to the bottom of the board. Continue layering waves upward. Take care to peel up the whale's tail to prevent covering it.

5 Attach individual waves around the whale's body. Have them point outward on either side.
  TIP: Once you've attached all of the waves, trim random waves with scissors so they don't all look the same.

6 Create and attach the right fin and right half of the bottom fin by covering fin-shaped cardboard in black duct tape. Attach the shapes to the canvas using smaller strips of duct tape.

Chapter 5
On the Go

Up until now, I've proved to you that you can not only wear duct tape, but that you can create thoughtful gifts with it, as well as use it to decorate your abode. In this final chapter, you'll find projects for letting duct tape work for you when you're on the go.

Weatherproof and durable, these duct tape projects barely scratch the surface of the ways you can include duct tape in your daily activities, whether it's during a commute to work, to school or a much-needed vacation.

Do you need a new lunch bag? We can handle that. How about a map case for your cruiser bicycle? Perfect! A new luggage tag to replace the one destroyed by the TSA? Yep, it's all here in this section, and then some.

So start unrolling the tape so we can get you packed up to go!

Post-It Holder

I use sticky notes constantly, but they're not much fun to use when the pad looks like the cat's been batting it around. This cute little holder will keep a small Post-it Note Pad safe and sound in any purse or pocket.

MATERIALS LIST

cutting mat

craft knife

straightedge

duct tape: white, assorted colors

Velcro or snap

needle and thread

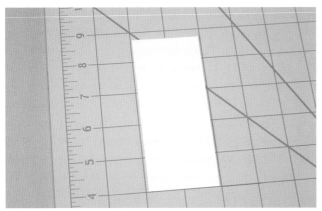

1 Create a 1⅞" × 4¾" (5cm × 12cm) double-sided piece of white fabric. (One side will be a single width of tape, and the other side will be three horizontal pieces.)

2 Wrap each of the seams with a small strip of tape to finish them off.

Wrap the fabric around a stack of Post-it Notes to find the folds and then burnish them.

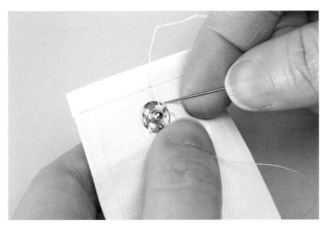

3 Attach a clasp on the front of the inside flap and on the back of the outside flap so the two flaps stay together. I sewed on a snap, but you could use a thin strip of Velcro so it's adjustable as the notes get used and replaced.

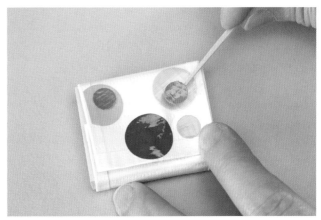

4 Embellish the front with various sizes and colors of duct tape dots.

Dots Journal

This durable little book makes a perfect travel journal. Use whatever paper you like for the text block: ruled to write on or watercolor paper to draw and paint on.

MATERIALS LIST

cutting mat

craft knife

straightedge

duct tape: white, teal, red

circles template (or die-cut system)

parchment paper

shrink plastic (or other flexible plastic), 2 pieces

8½" × 11" (22cm × 28cm) paper, 6 sheets

cardstock

corner rounder (optional)

needle or pushpin

waxed linen

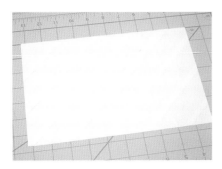

1 Create a 10¼" × 6¾" (26cm × 17cm) sheet of singled-sided white duct tape fabric. Adhere your tape together at a diagonal for an interesting effect.

2 Cut two 4½" × 5⅝" (11cm × 14cm) pieces of shrink plastic. Cover one side of each piece with blue tape and then round two of the corners on the same side.

3 Turn the white fabric over so the sticky side is facing up. Place the teal pieces on the white fabric, tape side up. Leave ⅜" (10mm) between the two plastic pieces and align the top and bottom edges.

4 Cover the whole piece in parchment and round the corners.

5 Remove the parchment. Place a ½" × 5⅝" (13mm × 14cm) strip of white tape down the center between the two blue pieces. The white piece will slightly overlap each blue piece.

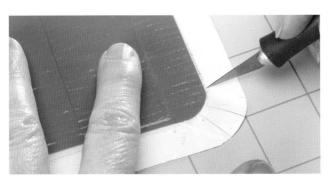

6 At the corners of the white fabric, cut small slits in the tape. This will help it fold more smoothly at the corners.

7 Fold the excess white up over the blue.

8 Fold six sheets of 8½" × 11" (22cm × 28cm) paper in half to create twelve 8½" × 5½" (22cm × 14cm) pages. Round the outside corners.

9 Separate them into two piles of three folded sheets each and stack them together, creating two signatures of paper.

10 Create a stitching guide on a piece of cardstock. Fold the paper in half and draw dots in the center. Twelve holes evenly spaced work well.

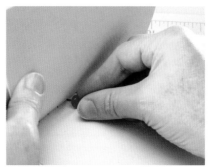

11 Place the cardstock in the center of one stack of paper. Using a needle or pushpin, punch a hole through the stack of paper at each drawn dot.

Repeat this step on the other stack of paper.

TIP: Keep the stack of paper folded while you punch the holes or they won't line up properly.

12 Create another stitch guide with two rows of twelve dots that match up with the stacks of paper (the rows should be about ¼" [6mm] apart). Place the stitch guide in the center of the white spine of the cover (between the two blue panels) and poke holes through the tape using a needle.

13 Thread a needle using a length of waxed linen or thread that is four times the height of the book.

TIP: Wrap the thread around the spine of the book twice to get the right length.

Line up the two signatures of paper with each row of holes in the spine of the cover. Starting with the top hole of the front signature, thread the needle from the center of the pages out through the cover. Leave a 6" (15cm) tail of thread on the inside.

Thread the needle through the top adjacent hole of the cover and then through the top hole of the back signature.

Thread the needle though the next hole on the back signature to the outside of the cover. Then go into the adjacent hole in the cover and through the second hole in the front signature.

Visit **artistsnetwork.com/ducttapediscovery** for more duct tape discoveries.

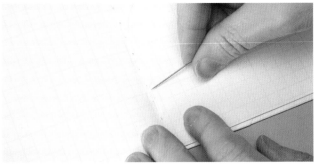

14 Continue back and forth between signatures as you work your way down the holes. Tie off when you reach the end.

15 Embellish the front with multiple sizes and colors of duct tape dot elements.

VARIATION

My friend Giuseppina "Josie" Cirincione created this beautiful journal by covering cardstock with duct tape for the covers and sewing it with a Japanese stab-binding technique. Josie used a Spellbinders cog die for the flowers.

Luggage Tag

Use bright colors for this tag so it's easier to spot your bag when it's on the baggage claim conveyor belt. I used a die-cut shape, but feel free to cut a simple rectangle or other shape.

MATERIALS LIST

cutting mat

craft knife

duct tape: teal, lime green, hot pink

parchment paper

clear shrink plastic (or other flexible plastic)

oval template

¼ " (6mm) hole punch

¼ " (6mm) eyelets

eyelet setter

hammer

paper

string or cord

1 Create a single layer of duct tape fabric that's at least 3½ " × 5 " (9cm × 13cm). Add a decorative strip of duct tape to the fabric. Place the fabric on parchment paper.

2 Cut a decorative border around the edges. Cut an oval shape out of the center of the tag that is 2¾" × 3¾" (7cm × 10cm).

3 Peel the parchment off. Create a plastic oval that is slightly larger than the hole you created. Place it over the hole on the sticky side of the tape. Set this piece aside.

4 Cut another piece of plastic in the same shape as one edge of the tag, but which leaves at least ¼" (6mm) of the sticky tape exposed on each side. Place it on the tape. This will allow the address paper to slide in and out of the tag.

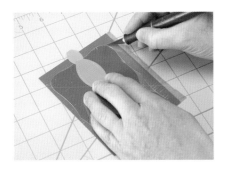

5 Create another single layer of duct tape fabric and trim the edges to match the front. Create one more single layer of duct tape fabric in the exact same way.

6 Taking care to match up the borders, connect the two solid pieces together.

7 Punch a hole through both layers at one edge. Grab the original piece with the oval cutout and punch a hole in the exact same spot. Set eyelets in each hole.

TIP: Place the oval cut tag on parchment paper while punching the hole so it won't stick to anything.

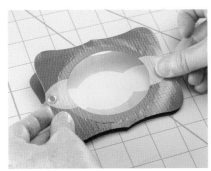

8 Attach the oval cut piece to the double-sided piece. Be sure to leave the plastic parts on the tape.

9 Cut a paper tag that is oval shaped at one end so it will fit inside. Be sure to punch a hole in the same place on this tag so it will match up with the eyelet holes.

10 Use a craft knife to trim any edges that don't meet exactly around the border of the tag. Write your name and contact information on the paper, slip it in the tag and run a string or cord through the holes.

Brushes Case

Although this case was designed for paintbrushes, it would also work for knitting needles or, on a smaller scale, makeup brushes. This project is great for packing up all of those wet brushes from a workshop.

MATERIALS LIST

cutting mat

craft knife

straightedge

duct tape: denim pattern, white, red

parchment paper

Velcro

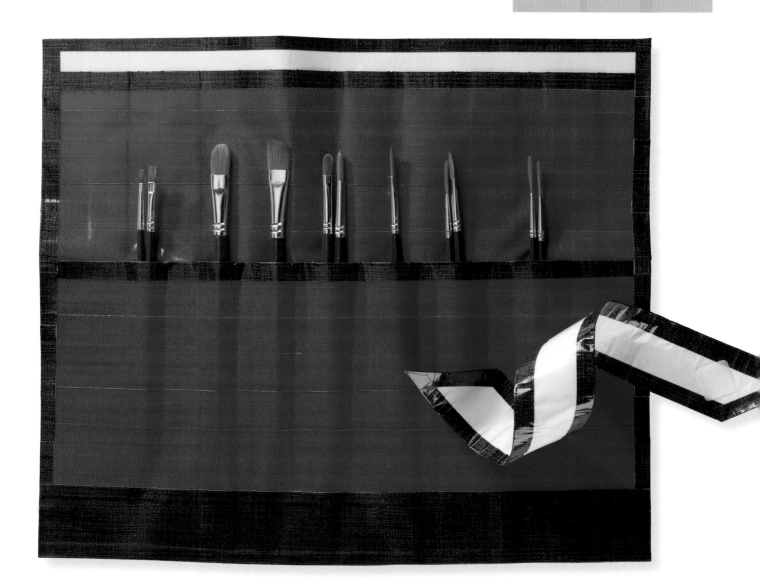

1 Create a 17" × 14¼"(43cm × 36cm) single-sided sheet of duct tape fabric using the denim tape. Cut a 16" (41cm) single strip of white duct tape. Center the white tape strip ½" (13mm) from one of the shorter denim tape's sticky sides.

2 Fold the ½" (13mm) denim tape edge over the white strip. Store this on a piece of parchment paper so you can set it aside.

3 Create a 16" × 12¾" (41cm × 32cm) single-sided sheet of red duct tape fabric. Cut eight strips of red duct tape. Two strips should be ¾" × 12¾" (19mm × 32cm); two strips at 1" × 12¾" (3cm × 32cm); two strips at 1⅛" × 12¾" (3cm × 32cm); and two strips at 1¼" × 12¾" (3cm × 32cm). Flip the red tape sheet over so the sticky side is up. Place the eight strips on the fabric, randomly spaced.

4 Cut a 17" (43cm) half-width strip of denim duct tape. Save the other half for later. Flip the red fabric over and attach the blue at the top. Flip the red sheet over again so the sticky side is up. Using a craft knife, cut slits in the denim strip at the end points of each red strip and fold the denim tabs onto the red strips.

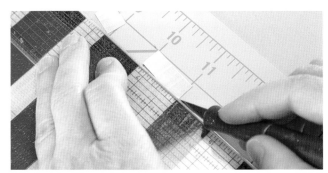

5 Remove the tabs of denim that overhang. *Do not* fold them over. Trim any excess red tape off the bottom of the fabric.

6 Remove the large denim fabric from the parchment paper and place the red sheet sticky side down on the adhesive of the denim sheet. Leave ½" (13mm) of the strip of white tape visible. Burnish the pieces together.

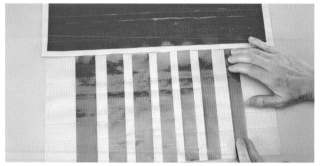

7 Create a 16" × 7¾" (41cm × 20cm) sheet of single-sided red tape fabric. Cut seven strips of red tape: four strips that are half-widths of the tape × 7¾" (20cm), two strips that are 1½" × 7¾" (4cm × 20cm) and one strip that is 1⅜" × 7¾" (3cm × 20cm). Line up the red fabric with the brush case. Position strips on the fabric between the strips on the case. This will ensure your brushes don't overlap when the case is finished.

8 Using the other half-width of the 17" (43cm) denim strip you made earlier, attach it to the top of the red fabric. Flip the fabric back over and cut tabs to fold on the red strips as you did in steps 4 and 5, and once again trim off the denim tape that is not folded over.

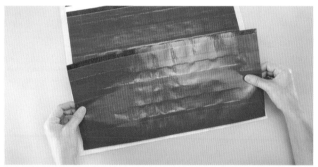

9 Line up the bottom of this sheet with the bottom of the red layer on the brush holder. Burnish the tape onto the brush holder.

10 Fold the denim border up around the red layers to secure them in place.

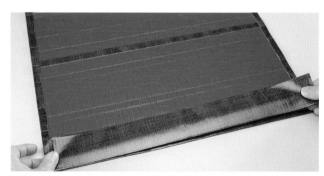

11 Cut a 17" (43cm) strip of denim and place it along the bottom of the holder.

12 Flip the brush holder over and add some embellishments on the front.

Visit **artistsnetwork.com/ducttapediscovery** for more duct tape discoveries.

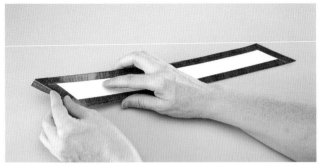

13 Cut a 16" (41cm) doubled-sided sheet of white fabric. Trim the ends at a 45-degree angle. Cut four half-width pieces of denim tape and wrap them around the white fabric edges to seal the seams.

14 Attach a piece of Velcro to each end of the wrap—one on the front, the other on the back.

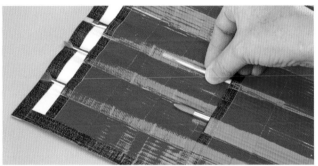

15 Insert brushes into the pockets.

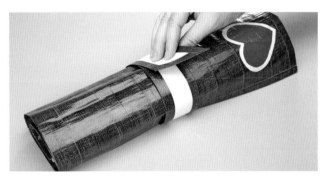

16 Roll up the case and use the belt to hold it together.

Lunch Sack

Based on the design of a simple brown paper sack, this bag folds up nice and flat when it's not in use. Because it's made of duct tape inside and out, spills are easy to clean. Embellish this bag to reflect your own style.

MATERIALS LIST

cutting mat

craft knife

straightedge

duct tape: orange, chocolate, white

permanent marker

scissors

Velcro

1 Create an 11" × 19" (28cm × 48cm) piece of double-sided duct tape fabric.

Visit **artistsnetwork.com/ducttapediscovery** for more duct tape discoveries.

2 Fold it in half and seal the sides using a 9½" (24cm) length of full-width tape.

3 Pleat the bottom corners like you would a paper bag and mark the 45-degree triangle at 3½" (9cm) from the tip.

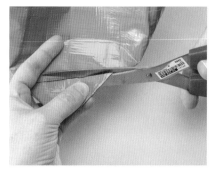

4 Cut off the triangle using scissors.

5 Seal the holes with small strips of tape. These will be covered more securely in the next step.

6 Cut an 11" × 3½" (28cm × 9cm) piece of matching fabric. Miter the corners at 45-degrees on each end to create a point. Adhere this to the bottom of the bag and fold the triangle flaps over the edges.
  Shape the sides by burnishing the corners.

7 Create a 7" × 6" (18cm × 15cm) piece of fabric for a flap. Two-thirds of the outside should be double-sided. Place the exposed part of the tape on the inside at the inside top of the bag.
  Flip the bag over and secure the flap on the outside with another piece of tape.

8 Seal the edges of the flap and the opening perimeter of the bag with strips of tape.

9 Embellish the flap with duct tape elements that match the rest of the bag.

10 Add Velcro to the bag and the inside of the flap so your lunch bag will stay closed.

Phone Case

Adjust the length of this strap as necessary, depending on your needs. And, yes, you can still operate the phone through the plastic front on the case. Did I mention the Batman tape glows in the dark?

MATERIALS LIST

cutting mat

craft knife

straightedge

duct tape: Batman, black

parchment paper

shrink plastic (or other flexible plastic), clear and black

⅛" (3mm) hole punch

⅛" (3mm) eyelets, 2

eyelet setter

hammer

industrial-strength Velcro

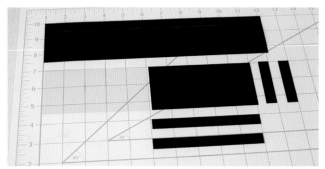

1 Create a single-sided piece of black duct tape fabric 11⅛" × 2½" (28cm × 6cm). Cut a piece of clear plastic 2½" × 4⅞" (6cm × 12cm) (front piece) and a piece of black shrink plastic at 2½" × 4⅞" (6cm × 12cm) (back piece). Cut two pieces of black plastic ½" × 2½" (13mm × 6cm) (top and bottom). Cut two pieces of black plastic ½" × 4⅞" (13mm × 12cm) (sides).

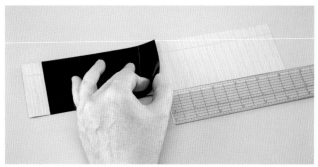

2 On the black strip of tape, place the black back piece of plastic 5⅜" (14cm) from one end of the tape.

3 Place the bottom piece of plastic on the short tape flap next to the large black plastic (leave a slit of space between the pieces). Fold the long black tape flap over the piece of black plastic.

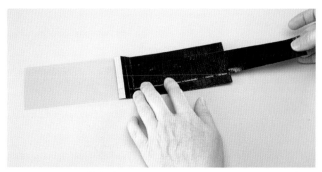

4 Cut a strip of black tape 10" × 1⅜" (25cm × 3cm). At the 4⅞" (12cm) point, notch two small lines with a craft knife but don't cut the tape entirely (⅛" [3mm] notches will do). Attach this to the tape-covered black plastic.

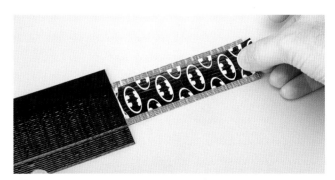

5 Flip this over and attach a length of Batman tape 4⅛" (10cm) to the exposed tape.

6 Fold the black tape around the Batman tape to finish the edges.

7 At 1⅞" (5cm) from the top of the black piece, punch two evenly spaced holes through the strap and through the tape-covered plastic.

8 Set an eyelet in each hole. I used bat-shaped eyelets to match the Batman theme.

9 Cut a piece of single-sided Batman fabric 4⅛" × 5¾" (10cm × 15cm). Notch ¾" (19mm) squares out of each bottom corner. Cut out a space at the top to fit around the strap.

10 Attach the Batman fabric to the outside of the case. Allow the strap to fit in the large notch at the top of the Batman fabric.

11 Flip the case over and lay the two side pieces on the Batman tape flaps almost flush with the black center piece (leave a sliver of space between). Fold the bottom and clear part around to the front. Pull up the bottom and each side and wrap the tape flaps around the clear plastic to keep the box together.

12 Cut a piece of Batman tape 2½" × 1⅞" (6cm × 5cm). Cut a piece of black tape 2⅞" × 1½" (7cm × 4cm). Place Batman tape at ¼" (6mm) from the top of the clear plastic on the outside.

Visit artistsnetwork.com/ducttapediscovery for more duct tape discoveries.

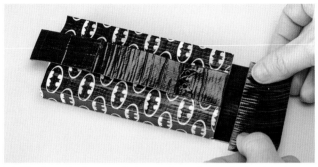

13 Place the last small plastic piece almost flush with the clear plastic on the tape. Cover the plastic and the exposed tape with the piece of black tape.

14 Cut slits in the corners of the black tape and wrap the flaps around the Batman tape to finish the seams.

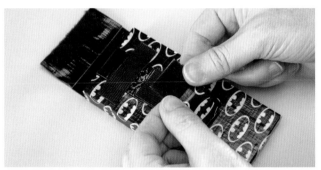

15 Attach strips of Velcro to the back and the flap. Attach Velcro to the top of the strap and the bottom of the underside of the strap so it rolls up. (Look for industrial-strength Velcro.)

DETAIL

Phone Bag

Although a smartphone is small enough to fit in your back pocket, carrying a cute bag is a lot more fun. Alternatively, this bag could easily double as an amulet bag. Channel your inner Bohemian.

MATERIALS LIST

cutting mat

craft knife

straightedge

duct tape: white, teal, pastel blue, lilac

parchment paper

white shrink plastic (or other flexible plastic)

¼" (6mm) eyelets, 2

¼" (6mm) hole punch

eyelet setter

hammer

Velcro

Visit **artistsnetwork.com/ducttapediscovery** for more duct tape discoveries.

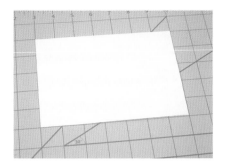

1 Create a 7" × 5" (18cm × 13cm) sheet of single-sided white duct tape fabric.

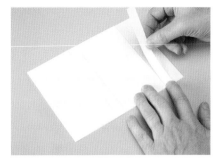

2 Cut two pieces of 2⅝" × 5" (7cm × 13cm) plastic. Cut two pieces of ½" × 5" (13mm × 13cm) plastic.

3 Place the plastic on the sticky side of the tape. Alternate the plastic pieces: large piece, small piece, large piece, small piece. Some sticky tape should remain exposed at one end.

4 Create two 2⅛" × 6" (5cm × 15cm) pieces of single-sided white fabric. Place them centered over the two large pieces of plastic to cover them. Fold the panels into a box and secure the box with the tape flap that is on one end.

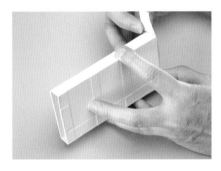

5 Cut a ½" × 2⅛" (13mm × 5cm) piece of plastic and attach it to one of the bottom flaps. Cut the other flap off. Cut a 5⅛" × ½" (13cm × 13mm) piece of white tape and cover the bottom to seal the corners.

6 At the top, fold each flap outward so there is still an opening. Using the Phone Bag Small Flap Template, cut a piece of white fabric. Most of this should be double-sided but leave a 1" (3cm) section (the part that isn't rounded) single-sided. Attach this flap to the inside of the square case.

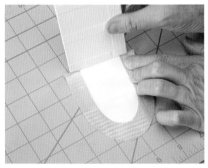

7 Create a purple single-sided flap using the Phone Bag Large Flap Template. Cut out the center part. Position the *U* shape around the edge of the white flap.

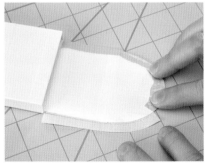

8 Flip the box over and press the excess purple down around the edge.

TIP: Cut small lines in the excess so it neatly folds around the curve.

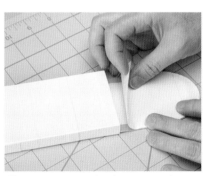

9 Cut a 3½" × 2⅛" (9cm × 5cm) single-sided white flap and round it to conform with the existing flap. Place it on the inside of the flap to cover the purple.

10 Cut a 7½" × 2⅛" (19cm × 5cm) piece of single-sided white fabric. Cover the back of the box and leave the excess hanging off the bottom. (Cover it with parchment paper to keep it from sticking to things.)

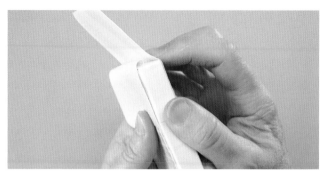

11 Cut another 7" × 2⅛" (18cm × 5cm) piece of single-sided white fabric to cover the front. Again leave the bottom hanging off the bottom. Carefully wrap each piece around the bottom edges. In the place where they meet at the center of the box bottom, adhere them together. This flap will be used to create a fringe hanging.

12 Trim the fringe hanging as needed to make it even along the bottom. Cut the fringe hanging into small strips of fringe using a craft knife. Make cuts about ⅛" (3mm) apart.

13 Embellish the front flap with duct tape elements of your choice. I used teal triangles and pastel blue squares.

14 Cut two ½" × 6" (13mm × 15cm) strips of single-sided white tape. Cut two ½" × 2" (13mm × 5cm) strips of single-sided white tape. Round the top of one end of each piece. Cover the strips with parchment to keep them from sticking to things and each other.

Cut two ½" × 1" (13mm × 3cm) pieces of plastic. Round one end of each piece to match the tape strips.

Attach a short piece of the tape to a long piece at the rounded edges and sandwich a piece of the plastic between the two. Be careful not to attach the whole short piece; just adhere it to the end of the plastic.

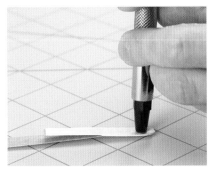

15 Punch a hole through the tape and plastic of each strip and then set an eyelet in each hole.

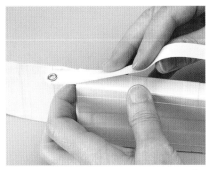

16 Attach the strips to each side of the box. The short strip should go inside the box, and the long strip should reach to the bottom of the box.

17 Cut three strands of different colored tape (match the tape to the colors of the bag), each 42 " (107cm) long. Roll each strand into a rounded cord. Thread all three strands through one of the eyelets and tie a knot.

Braid the three strands together and thread the three tails through the other eyelet. Tie the ends in a knot to secure the strap.

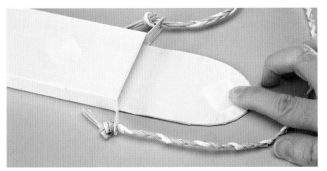

18 Add a strip of Velcro to the inside of the flap and the front of the bag.

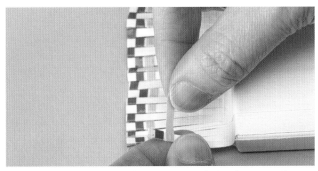

19 Create the effect of beads on the fringe by wrapping small pieces of duct tape around individual fringe pieces.

DETAIL

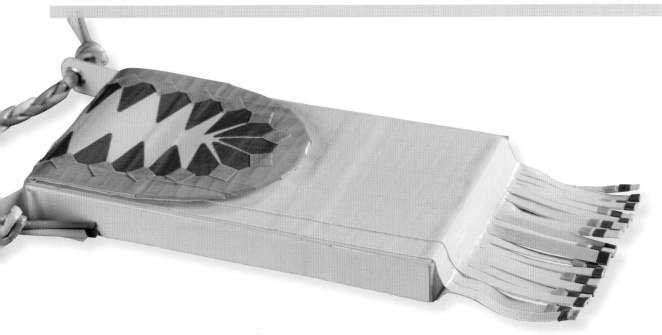

Cruiser Case

This project is inspired by a traditional bicycle map case. The straps secure the bag to the handlebars. While you may not rely on a paper map to ride, this bag is perfect for holding other small items.

MATERIALS LIST

cutting mat

craft knife

straightedge

duct tape: floral pattern, lime green, hot pink, assorted brights

paper

scissors

parchment paper

Velcro

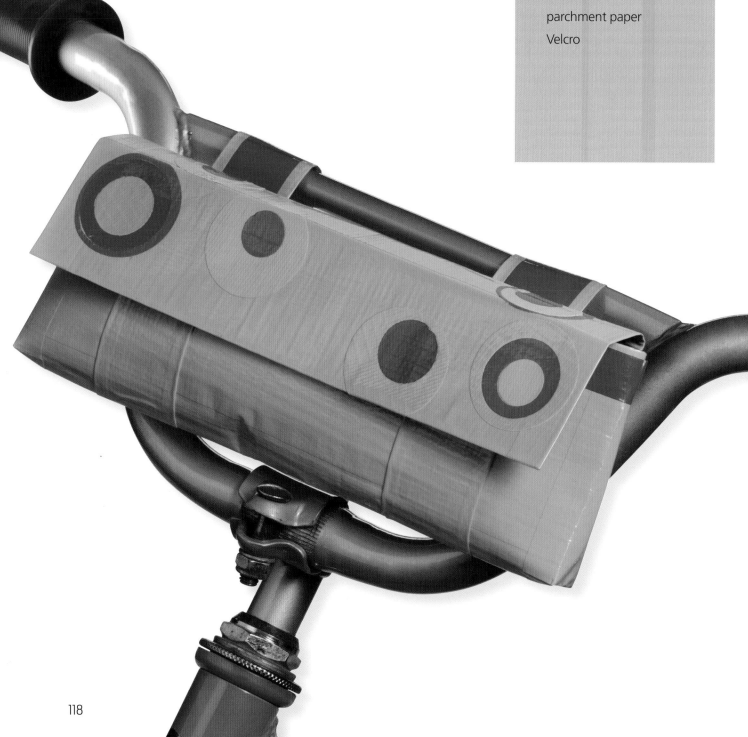

1 Create a 9½" × 7¾" (24cm × 20cm) double-sided piece of duct tape fabric. One side should be lime green; the other, flowered.

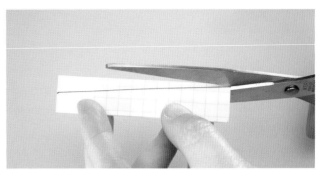

2 Fold a 3½"-long (9cm) paper in half and cut it at an angle to create a triangle with a base of ¾" (19mm) and a point at the top.

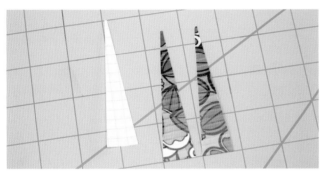

3 Unfold the paper triangle and use it to cut two triangles out of the flowered tape.

4 Attach the triangles to the centers of 5" (13cm) strips of lime green tape. The sticky sides should connect.

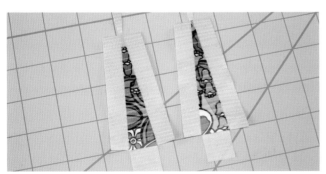

5 Cut out each of the corners as shown.

6 Fold the large fabric in half lengthwise to find the center. Position the fold at the bottom center of one of the triangles. Connect the pieces by meeting the flowered tape on the inside of the fabric to the flowered triangle. Wrap the lime green tape around the front to seal the sides.

7 Fold the thin top flap into the bag. Repeat steps 6 and 7 on the opposite side. Burnish the folds at the bottom and sides.

8 Create two sheets of 8⅞" × 4" (23cm × 10cm) single-sided fabric that match the inside and outside of the bag. Cover one long section of each piece with ½" (13mm) strips of parchment paper.

9 Stick the two pieces together. The parchment will prevent them from sealing all the way.

10 Remove the parchment on the green side and adhere it at the opening of the outside of the bag.

11 Remove the other strip of parchment and adhere it to the inside. You now have a flap for the case.

12 Cut two 11⅜" (29cm) strips of green tape. Center a 1¼" × 4¼" (3cm x 11cm) piece of pink tape about ¼" (6mm) from one edge of each green strip.

Visit **artistsnetwork.com/ducttapediscovery** for more duct tape discoveries.

"Love" Frame Template

Feather Cuff Template

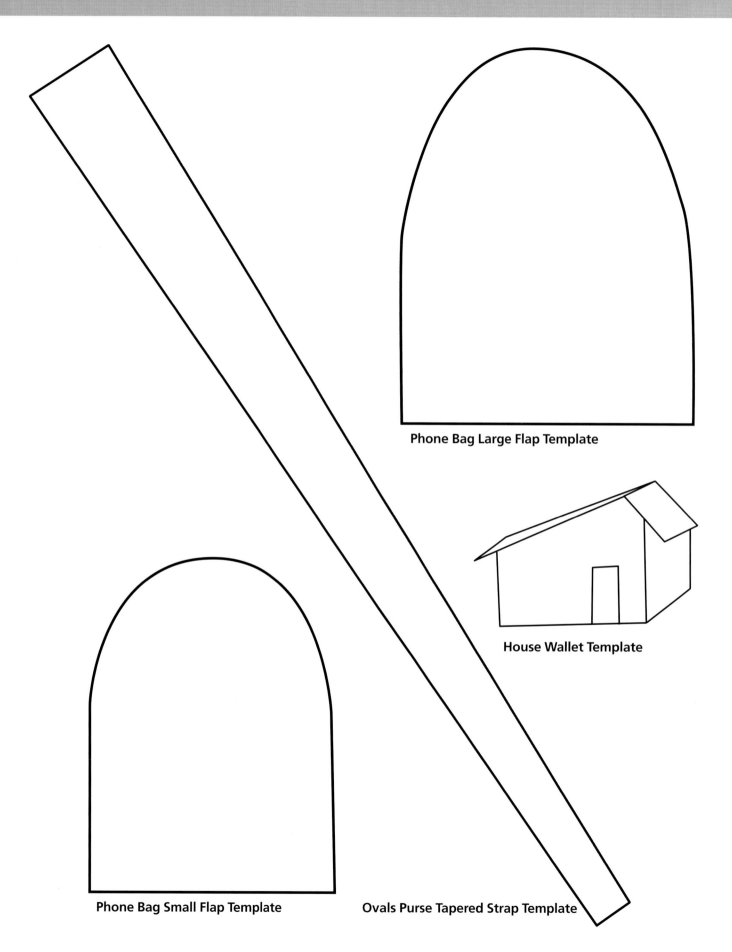

Phone Bag Large Flap Template

House Wallet Template

Phone Bag Small Flap Template

Ovals Purse Tapered Strap Template

About the Author

Tonia Jenny is the acquisitions editor and senior content developer for North Light Mixed Media. A mixed-media artist and jewelry designer herself, Tonia has authored two North Light books: *Frame It!* and *Plexi Class*. When she's not busy making art, cooking, reading or exploring new ways of looking at the world, you can find her on her bicycle or on Instagram.

Acknowledgments

Thanks for insisting I could write this book, Mona Clough! It turned out to be even more fun than I imagined. Thank you to my wonderful editor, Amy Jones; you made the process super easy and enjoyable for me. Christine Polomsky and Geoff Raker, the book wouldn't look this good without you! Thanks to the rest of the North Light team for each piece of the book you touched and for your ongoing support of my wacky ideas.

A very big thanks to Josie Cirincione, who was the first to suggest I cut shapes from duct tape using parchment paper. Without that solution, these projects wouldn't have been the same.

And a second big thanks to Ken Oliver and Spellbinders for letting me experiment with their dies. The dies sure make cutting shapes a breeze.

Dedication

To David: Thanks for putting up with all the hours I spent cutting and sticking things together and for supporting me in anything I dream up.

Index

Edited by
Amy Jones

Designed by
Geoff Raker

Photography by
Christine Polomsky
and **Kris Kandler**

Production coordinated by
Jennifer Bass

Other fine North Light Books are available from your favorite bookstore, art supply store or online supplier. Visit our website at fwmedia.com.

18 17 16 15 14   5 4 3 2 1

DISTRIBUTED IN CANADA BY FRASER DIRECT
100 Armstrong Avenue
Georgetown, ON, Canada L7G 5S4
Tel: (905) 877-4411

DISTRIBUTED IN THE U.K. AND EUROPE
BY F&W MEDIA INTERNATIONAL LTD
Brunel House, Forde Close, Newton Abbot, TQ12 4PU, UK
Tel: (+44) 1626 323200, Fax: (+44) 1626 323319
Email: enquiries@fwmedia.com

DISTRIBUTED IN AUSTRALIA BY CAPRICORN LINK
P.O. Box 704, S. Windsor NSW, 2756 Australia
Tel: (02) 4560-1600; Fax: (02) 4577 5288
Email: books@capricornlink.com.au

ISBN 13: 978-1-4403-3395-8

fw
media

Metric Conversion Chart

To convert	to	multiply by
Inches	Centimeters	2.54
Centimeters	Inches	0.4
Feet	Centimeters	30.5
Centimeters	Feet	0.03
Yards	Meters	0.9
Meters	Yards	1.1

Ideas. Instruction. Inspiration.

Receive FREE downloadable bonus materials when you sign up for our free newsletter at artistsnetwork.com/Newsletter_Thanks.

Find the latest issues of *Cloth Paper Scissors* on newsstands, or visit shop.clothpaperscissors.com.

 These and other fine North Light products are available at your favorite art and craft retailer, bookstore or online supplier. Visit our websites at artistsnetwork.com and artistsnetwork.tv.

 Follow North Light Books for the latest news, free wallpapers, free demos and chances to win FREE BOOKS!

Visit artistsnetwork.com and get Jen's North Light Picks!

Get free step-by-step demonstrations along with reviews of the latest books, videos and downloads from Jennifer Lepore, senior editor and online education manager at North Light Books.

Get involved
Learn from the experts. Join the conversation on